OPPOSING
VIEWPOINTS®
SERIES

Food

Date Due

NOV 0 1 2006			
NOV 1 1 2007			
NOV 2 6 2012			
OCT 1 6 2014			

Other Books of Related Interest:

At Issue Series

Fast Food

Food Safety

Genetically Engineered Foods

Is Factory Farming Harming America?

Contemporary Issues Companion Series

Eating Disorders

Genetic Engineering

Current Controversies Series

Biodiversity

Genetic Engineering

Opposing Viewpoints Series

Genetic Engineering

Health

Obesity

"Congress shall make no law . . . abridging the freedom of speech, or of the press."

First Amendment to the U.S. Constitution

The basic foundation of our democracy is the First Amendment guarantee of freedom of expression. The Opposing Viewpoints Series is dedicated to the concept of this basic freedom and the idea that it is more important to practice it than to enshrine it.

Food

Laura K. Egendorf, Book Editor

GREENHAVEN PRESS

An imprint of Thomson Gale, a part of The Thomson Corporation

Detroit • New York • San Francisco • New Haven, Conn. • Waterville, Maine • London • Munich

Bonnie Szumski, *Publisher*
Helen Cothran, *Managing Editor*

© 2006 Thomson Gale, a part of The Thomson Corporation.

Thomson and Star Logo are trademarks and Gale and Greenhaven Press are registered trademarks used herein under license.

For more information, contact:
Greenhaven Press
27500 Drake Rd.
Farmington Hills, MI 48331-3535
Or you can visit our Internet site at http://www.gale.com

LIBRARY OF CONGRESS CATALOGING-IN-PUBLICATION DATA

Food / Laura K. Egendorf, book editor.
    p. cm. -- (Opposing viewpoints)
    Includes bibliographical references and index.
    ISBN 0-7377-3232-6 (pbk. : alk. paper) -- ISBN 0-7377-3231-8 (lib. : alk. paper)
    1. Terrorism--United States. 2. Food supply--United States. 3. Animal industry--United States. 4. Agriculture--United States. 5. Obesity--United States. 6. Hunger--United States. I. Egendorf, Laura K., 1973– II. Opposing viewpoints series (Unnumbered)
    HV6432.F64 2006
    363.80973--dc22
                                             2006043357

Printed in the United States of America
10 9 8 7 6 5 4 3 2 1

Contents

Chapter 3: What Causes Obesity?

Chapter 4: How Can Hunger Be Reduced?

Why Consider Opposing Viewpoints?

> "The only way in which a human being can make some approach to knowing the whole of a subject is by hearing what can be said about it by persons of every variety of opinion and studying all modes in which it can be looked at by every character of mind. No wise man ever acquired his wisdom in any mode but this."
>
> *John Stuart Mill*

In our media-intensive culture it is not difficult to find differing opinions. Thousands of newspapers and magazines and dozens of radio and television talk shows resound with differing points of view. The difficulty lies in deciding which opinion to agree with and which "experts" seem the most credible. The more inundated we become with differing opinions and claims, the more essential it is to hone critical reading and thinking skills to evaluate these ideas. Opposing Viewpoints books address this problem directly by presenting stimulating debates that can be used to enhance and teach these skills. The varied opinions contained in each book examine many different aspects of a single issue. While examining these conveniently edited opposing views, readers can develop critical thinking skills such as the ability to compare and contrast authors' credibility, facts, argumentation styles, use of persuasive techniques, and other stylistic tools. In short, the Opposing Viewpoints Series is an ideal way to attain the higher-level thinking and reading skills so essential in a culture of diverse and contradictory opinions.

In addition to providing a tool for critical thinking, Opposing Viewpoints books challenge readers to question their own strongly held opinions and assumptions. Most people form their opinions on the basis of upbringing, peer pressure, and personal, cultural, or professional bias. By reading carefully balanced opposing views, readers must directly confront new ideas as well as the opinions of those with whom they disagree. This is not to simplistically argue that everyone who reads opposing views will—or should—change his or her opinion. Instead, the series enhances readers' understanding of their own views by encouraging confrontation with opposing ideas. Careful examination of others' views can lead to the readers' understanding of the logical inconsistencies in their own opinions, perspective on why they hold an opinion, and the consideration of the possibility that their opinion requires further evaluation.

Evaluating Other Opinions

To ensure that this type of examination occurs, Opposing Viewpoints books present all types of opinions. Prominent spokespeople on different sides of each issue as well as well-known professionals from many disciplines challenge the reader. An additional goal of the series is to provide a forum for other, less known, or even unpopular viewpoints. The opinion of an ordinary person who has had to make the decision to cut off life support from a terminally ill relative, for example, may be just as valuable and provide just as much insight as a medical ethicist's professional opinion. The editors have two additional purposes in including these less known views. One, the editors encourage readers to respect others' opinions—even when not enhanced by professional credibility. It is only by reading or listening to and objectively evaluating others' ideas that one can determine whether they are worthy of consideration. Two, the inclusion of such viewpoints encourages the important critical thinking skill of objectively evaluating an author's credentials and bias. This evaluation will illuminate an author's reasons for taking a particular stance on an issue and will aid in readers' evaluation of the author's ideas.

It is our hope that these books will give readers a deeper understanding of the issues debated and an appreciation of the complexity of even seemingly simple issues when good and honest people disagree. This awareness is particularly important in a democratic society such as ours in which people enter into public debate to determine the common good. Those with whom one disagrees should not be regarded as enemies but rather as people whose views deserve careful examination and may shed light on one's own.

Thomas Jefferson once said that "difference of opinion leads to inquiry, and inquiry to truth." Jefferson, a broadly educated man, argued that "if a nation expects to be ignorant and free . . . it expects what never was and never will be." As individuals and as a nation, it is imperative that we consider the opinions of others and examine them with skill and discernment. The Opposing Viewpoints Series is intended to help readers achieve this goal.

David L. Bender and Bruno Leone,
Founders

Introduction

> *"Maybe what we should be talking about is an American paradox: that is, a notably unhealthy people obsessed by the idea of eating healthily."*
>
> —*Michael Pollan,*
> *journalism professor*

The American attitude toward food is filled with contradictions. Americans eat "home-style" meals in restaurants because they are too busy to make similar meals at home. They spend virtually the same amount of money on remodeling kitchens as they do on diet products. The average American is overweight, yet eating disorders remain common among young women. Americans eagerly read about which foods to consume and which to avoid, but after reading the articles many drive to the nearest fast-food restaurant for lunch. These contradictions point to a society that is alternately obsessed with and fearful of food.

Millions of Americans suffer from one of two opposing conditions—obesity and eating disorders. Obesity is perhaps the most serious health problem facing the United States, as people who are severely overweight face increased risks of heart disease, asthma, and diabetes. Approximately one-third of American adults are obese, defined as being at least thirty pounds above the healthy weight for their height. Another third are overweight. In addition, 15 percent of school-age children are overweight. The health problems associated with obesity are frequently fatal. Surgeon General Richard H. Carmona declared before a congressional subcommittee in 2003 that more than three hundred thousand Americans would die that year from illnesses relating to being overweight or obese.

He notes, "One out of every eight deaths in America is caused by an illness directly related to overweight and obesity." However, being heavy is not the only weight-related danger for Americans; being underweight can be equally deadly. Eleven million Americans, mostly teenage girls and women in their twenties, suffer from the eating disorders anorexia and bulimia. Approximately one thousand people die from complications from anorexia each year.

Concerns about weight are also manifested in Americans' obsession with dieting. The U.S. diet industry is a $46-billion business; as many as 80 million American adults are on a diet at any given time. Diets such as Atkins and the Zone receive enormous media attention because of their claims of immediate results. Paradoxically, dieting causes Americans to believe that they eat more healthily than they actually do. As market researcher Kris Hodges observes in an article she wrote for *American Demographics*, "Nearly 1 in 4 Americans (23 percent) is over-confident of their caloric intake, believing the number of calories they consume is about right, while in reality they're overweight or obese."

One of the reasons Americans are overweight is because of the meals they eat outside the home. Nutritionists note that it is more difficult to control portion size and calorie content if the food is prepared by someone else. Five hundred billion dollars were spent nationwide in restaurants in 2004. At the same time, while Americans were eating more meals outside the home, they spent $47 billon on kitchen remodeling and $333 million on cookbooks that same year. In essence, Americans seem to love the idea of cooking at home but are more likely to eat out or buy ready-to-serve meals. In a December 2005 article in the *New York Times*, food stylist Andrew Scrivani observes, Americans "optimistically purchase [TV chef] Emeril [Lagasse's] cookware, download [chef] Daniel

[Boulod's] recipes and watch cooking shows. Yet they eat breakfast in their cars, lunch at their desks and chicken from a bucket."

Americans' paradoxical attitudes toward food illustrate a love affair with eating and an obsession with health and thinness. In *Opposing Viewpoints: Food* the authors consider many issues related to food in the following chapters: Is America's Food Supply Safe? How Should Farms Be Operated? What Causes Obesity? How Can Hunger Be Reduced? The viewpoints in this volume highlight a number of contradictions related to food: the presence of both hunger and obesity in the world, the push for organic food production at the same time that genetically modified crops are becoming increasingly popular, and a movement to replace large factory farms with small, local farms when demand for food is increasing due to an expanding world population. Americans are clearly not the only people conflicted about food.

OPPOSING
VIEWPOINTS®
SERIES

CHAPTER 1

Is America's Food Supply Safe?

Chapter Preface

When he left office at the end of 2004, Department of Health and Human Services secretary Tommy Thompson reiterated a concern that he had expressed several times during his tenure. According to Thompson, America's food supply was inadequately protected against a potential terrorist attack. In remarks he made after announcing his resignation, Thompson commented, "I, for the life of me, cannot understand why the terrorists have not attacked our food supply, because it is so easy to do." Such attacks could include dusting crops with deadly chemicals or poisoning prepared foods. Although not everyone agrees with Thompson's assessment, many commentators assert that steps must be taken to ensure that the nation's food is not attacked by terrorists.

Although they have not occurred on a large scale, terrorist attacks on the food supply have happened. At least five such acts have occurred in the United States, including an outbreak of salmonella poisoning in Oregon in 1984, which caused over seven hundred people to fall ill. The attack was linked to a cult that wanted to overthrow the county government. A more recent attack occurred in Canada in 2000, when twenty-seven people were poisoned with arsenic-laced coffee in Quebec City. If these acts of terrorism were to succeed on a large scale, they would, according to science writers Joseph Dudley and Michael Woodford, "[cause] high levels of mortality or morbidity." Terrorist attacks on the food supply could also wreak havoc on the economy and cause distrust of the government.

Government agencies and commentators have offered various opinions on how best to secure America's food supply. The Food and Drug Administration (FDA), which is responsible for the safety of 80 percent of the U.S. food supply, explains its efforts in its publication, *FDA Consumer*. According to Michelle Meadows, a staff writer for the magazine, the FDA aims to improve food security by working with federal, state, and local officials, identifying potential attacks, and preparing vaccines and other medical countermeasures. Other counterterrorism measures that have been suggested include improving monitoring systems and educating farms and consumers.

However, some people believe that agricultural terrorism will never become a serious threat. In an analysis published in the *Bulletin of the Atomic Scientists*, Gavin Cameron, Jason Pate, and Kathleen Vogel contend that "the threat may not be as dire as alarmists claim." They assert that of the twenty-one terrorist incidents in the twentieth century that might be deemed attacks on agriculture, almost all were small in scale, and several could be classified as regular crimes rather than violent political acts. They claim that most terrorists lack the scientific knowledge and resources to successfully harm America's plants and animals. However, Cameron, Pate, and Vogel warn that the media and politicians may be encouraging agricultural terrorism by publicizing the possibility.

Although a large-scale agricultural terrorist attack on the United States has not happened, the possibility of such a strike adds to concerns about the safety of the American food supply. Other potential threats discussed in this chapter include mad cow disease and genetically modified crops.

"*[Mad cow] disease could be incubating inside millions—or even hundreds of millions—of meat-eaters.*"

Mad Cow Disease Threatens Human Health

Hightower Lowdown

In the following viewpoint the newsletter Hightower Lowdown *asserts that bovine spongiform encephalopathy—more commonly known as mad cow disease—can infect humans, causing part of their brains to become spongelike. According to the publication, the U.S. Department of Agriculture tests a very small amount of cattle, thus increasing the likelihood that the fatal brain disease will go undetected. The newsletter further argues that the political power of the beef industry has made the government unwilling to ensure the safety of American beef.* Hightower Lowdown *is a monthly political newsletter edited by former politician Jim Hightower and political writer Phillip Frazer.*

As you read, consider the following questions:

1. How many cattle are tested each year for mad cow disease, according to the newsletter?

2. What percentage of people with Alzheimer's have been misdiagnosed, as noted by the newsletter?

Hightower Lowdown, "BushCo's Mad, Mad, Mad, Mad Mad Cow Policy," *Hightower Lowdown*, edited by Jim Hightower and Phillip Frazer, vol. 6, April 2004, pp. 1-4. Copyright © 2004, Public Intelligence, Inc. Reproduced by permission of Jim Hightower, The Hightower Lowdown, December 2005, www.hightowerlowdown.org.

3. According to *Hightower Lowdown*, how many cattle may be infected by 2015?

When the first undeniable American case of Mad Cow Disease broke into the news [in December 2003], a host of Bush officials trotted out to shout reassurances at us: "Just an isolated case!" ... "America's beef supply is the safest in the world!" ... "Trust us, we're experts!" Even George W. told the media that he'd eaten a big serving of beef for Christmas dinner—see, no problem, all clean, don't think about it any more.

Yes, admitted the [Agriculture] Department's top animal scientist, the mad cow in question was part of a herd of 80 cattle that could also be infected, but, by gollies, our animal tracking system is excellent, so "we feel confident that we are going to be able to determine the whereabouts of most, if not all, of these animals within the next several days." Trust us.

Seven weeks later, the Ag Department scientist had to admit that only one-third of the suspect cattle could be found. "We never expected to be able to find all of them," he lied in classic Bushite fashion, apparently hoping that we wouldn't recall his earlier promise. The other two-thirds couldn't be tracked and presumably had ended up in our lunches and dinners. Declaring the investigation over, he said, "It's time to move on."

Move on? To where? To a Mad Cow burger? To the intensive care unit? So much for our "experts."

Ignoring the Experts

When real experts do speak, the Bushites cover their ears. Ag Secretary Ann Veneman had attempted to calm public concern last December by convening a panel of international experts on Mad Cow Disease, expecting the members to do little more than a cursory review of the beef industry's production system and then rubber-stamp the industry's mantra that

America has no Mad Cow problem, that the government's safety rules are more than adequate to protect consumers.

But—Holy Big Mac!—the panel bolted. In remarkably direct language, Ann's rebellious experts found that Mad Cow Disease is common in our cattle herds, that the USDA's [U.S. Department of Agriculture's] voluntary tracking system is grossly inadequate, and that the meat industry's method of feeding rendered parts of hogs, chickens, goats, road kill (yes, road kill), and other animals to cattle (which, by nature, are not carnivores at all, but grass-grazing vegetarians—vegans, even) is inherently unsafe.

The experts also concluded that the reason the USDA has found only this one case of Mad Cow Disease so far is that it hasn't been looking very hard. Of the 30 million cattle slaughtered each year, only 40,000 are tested for the deadly disease, barely one-tenth of one percent. The panel chairman said that USDA might find "a case a month" of Mad Cow if it was doing enough testing.

A Powerful Industry

The Bushites and industry, which are always lecturing environmentalists and consumers that "science, not politics" should be the sole basis for making regulatory policy, responded to this scientific finding by what else?—resorting to pure politics. Industry lobbyists rushed to the media to blindly reiterate the absurd and thoroughly unscientific claim that Mad Cow "poses no risk to consumers." A top lobbying group, apparently auditioning for *Saturday Night Live*, complained that the scientists' report was "negative in tone" (well, duh, yeah—it's hard to be upbeat about the probability of Mad Cow in our Happy Meals). This same group, the National Cattlemen's Beef Association, then invoked the Bushonian Gospel, asserting that the best policy in these situations was for government to continue its benign neglect by "letting industry address these things."

Did I mention that meat processors and corporate cattle operators have put nearly a million bucks into Bush's presidential campaign? The Bushites can talk about "science" until the cows come home, but their policies are all about politics.

The Facts About Mad Cow

Despite the official shuck and jive, the basic facts about Mad Cow Disease are not in dispute:

- It has infected thousands of animals in England in the past decade, and more recently has spread to other countries, leading to the destruction of millions of cattle;

- Eighty-eight people are known to have died from the human variant of Mad Cow Disease in England, four in the rest of Europe, two are dying in Thailand, and three Americans have died after eating elk or deer probably infected with a version of the disease, possibly after the animals were fed processed food pellets that included rendered cow parts.

- Officially, no person in the U.S. has contracted the human version of Mad Cow, but many experts now say the disease could be incubating inside millions—or even hundreds of millions—of meat-eaters here and elsewhere the world over (once ingested, it can take 40 years for Mad Cow to appear in the eater).

- No amount of cooking, freezing, pickling, irradiation, drying, or smoking will protect against this contaminated meat.

Opportunities for Contamination

On NBC's *Today*, USDA Secretary Veneman insisted "the fact of the matter is that all scientific evidence would show, based upon what we know about this disease, that muscle cuts—that is, the meat of the animal itself—should not cause any risk to human health."

This statement directly contradicts a 2002 report from the U.S. General Accounting Office (GAO), the investigative arm of Congress, which states: "In terms of the public health risk, consumers do not always know when foods and other products they use may contain central nervous system tissue. . . . Many edible products, such as beef stock, beef extract, and beef flavoring, are frequently made by boiling the skeletal remains (including the vertebral column) of the carcass. . . . "

According to another watchdog group, the Center for Science in the Public Interest, spinal-cord contamination may also be found in US hot dogs, hamburgers, pizza toppings, and taco fillings. In fact, a 2002 USDA survey showed that approximately 35% of high-risk meat products tested positive for central-nervous-system tissues.

The GAO report continues: "In light of the experiences in Japan and other countries that were thought to be BSE-free, we believe that it would be prudent for USDA to consider taking some action to inform consumers when products may contain central nervous system or other tissue that could pose a risk if taken from a BSE-infected cow."

The Alzheimer's Connection

Not only do American cows have this horrific disease, but there's distressing evidence that American people do, too. Consider the Alzheimer's connection.

Alzheimer's disease, little known just a generation ago, is now so common in our land that the term has come to be used as a joke, as in: "Excuse me for forgetting your name—I'm having an Alzheimer's moment."

Of course, Alzheimer's is no joke, but a cruel and fatal disease that essentially dissolves the brain, causing victims literally to lose their minds. Alzheimer's has been surging in

A Too Generous Threshold

Instead of resolving to find every case of mad cow disease and eradicate it from the United States, the USDA [U.S. Department of Agriculture] [has] engaged in a how-much-is-too-much conversation in which it balanced the safety of our meat supply with the beef industry's bottom line.

That cost-benefit approach is how regulatory Washington makes decisions these days, and the mad cow fiasco is the perfect example of the moral bankruptcy of the method. With 36 million cattle slaughtered annually in the United States, "one-in-a-million" threshold would actually allow more than one case of mad cow disease every two weeks.

Frank Ackerman and Lisa Heinzerling,
Los Angeles Times, *February 26, 2004.*

America over the past two decades: It's now registered as the eighth leading cause of death, afflicting some four million of our people.

But there's one aspect of this that the economic and political powers that be in our country don't want scientists discussing in public. Autopsy studies done at Yale and elsewhere show that 20 percent of people diagnosed with Alzheimer's were misdiagnosed: They actually had another brain-wasting disease called Creutzfeldt-Jakob Disease (CJD), and thousands of these cases might well be a variant of CJD caused by Mad Cow-infected meat that the victims had eaten years earlier.

Yes, this means that Mad Cow Disease in humans, which the beef industry has adamantly insisted does not exist at all in America, could actually be widespread and already killing people under another name. . . .

Reforming the System

Beef is a huge business in America. There are more than 100 million cattle in the US at present, and meat and milk sales produce approximately $54 billion a year, with more than $100 billion in related services and industries. This is not an industry that wants any whisper of a deadly contamination in its products. Yet rather than clean up its act, it uses its political clout to put the hush-hush on reality.

Fortunately, an unlikely coalition of pure-food groups, scientists, consumer advocates, foreign-trade representatives and even small meat processors themselves kept pounding away at the USDA's mad Mad Cow policy until Ms. Veneman finally had to blink. The Ag Department announced in mid-March that it will increase tenfold the testing for Mad Cow Disease, including half of the nation's 446,000 "downer" cows. It will also test 20,000 older, apparently healthy cows at slaughter.

That's an improvement, but keep in mind that by no means does this new testing ensure that every cow is clean—99% of cows will still not be tested.

Even this small increase in testing might not have happened if not for Tom Ellestead. He's an owner of the plant in Moses Lake, Washington, where America's first mad cow was found. Contrary to the USDA's claim that this was a downer cow, Ellestead has signed an affidavit stating that the cow appeared healthy at the time of slaughter and was tested by accident. Meaning, of course, that if a "healthy" cow can have Mad Cow, how many other "healthy" animals have escaped detection and found their way into our food supply? Ellestead bluntly says that, rather than create a nationwide panic, the USDA inspector changed the paperwork to say that the cow in question was a downer cow.

Ignoring the Dangers

Amid the swirling controversy, Secretary Veneman announced that even the modest new steps toward reform would begin not today or tomorrow ... but in a few months!

I feel safer already. Don't you? If you squeeze your mind shut real tight, you might be able to keep from thinking about all the untested cows that will have been killed and eaten between last December and this coming June, when the new testing begins. Or you might keep from thinking about the 251,000 cows that, according to the USDA, died in 2002 due to unknown reasons, or for reasons that could be consistent with BSE-related clinical signs. Or you might put out of mind the rendered dairy cows that are still fed to American pigs—and the rendered pig carcasses that are, in turn, fed back to cows. Or the fact that chickens are fed beef parts, and that chicken manure is then scooped up and (sorry to have to tell you this) fed back to cows. Or about the various bodily fluids and gelatin from cows that are still used in a wide variety of processed-food products, despite the likelihood of containing nerve tissue. Or the . . . you get the idea.

Even if rendered feed was banned today, as many as 299,000 infected cattle could be expected in the following 11 years. That would be due to the latency period of up to 10 years before Mad Cow Disease manifests in animals. The latency period for the human form of the illness, the always-fatal variant CJD, is five to 40 years after eating infected meat.

Three Steps to Take

Three minimal steps should be taken immediately to learn the full truth and to protect public health.

1. The USDA should test *all* cattle—as Japan does as a matter of course. At the behest of Tyson and the other big beef purveyors, the Bushites have rejected this move.

2. USDA should ban the feeding of any and all slaughterhouse waste to cattle. While the agency has finally banned feeding cattle parts to cattle (yes—cow cannibalism!), those cattle parts are still fed to hogs, chickens, etc., which in turn are fed to cattle. It's

second-hand cannibalism, and it can pass Mad Cow Disease right through to your child's burger. Secretary Veneman has rejected this zero-tolerance ban on cow cannibalism, however, not wishing to inconvenience the beef purveyors.

3. There should be a national monitoring system of all CJD cases in humans to determine the extent that Mad Cow infection is involved. This is no big deal, for doctors routinely monitor and report on all sorts of other diseases so medical science can know what it's dealing with. Again, the beef purveyors have said no.

Over the long term, we should take a cue from the European Union's [EU's] Agriculture, Rural Development and Fisheries Commissioner, Franz Fischler, who backs a German plan to reshape agriculture toward "eco-farming." The EU and the German government are shifting subsidies from meat and bulk cereals to environmental services for farmers, extensive livestock farming and organic farming.

Finally, keep in mind that the extent of the risk of human infection is likely to remain unknown for some time. You need to make a judgment call. If you want to eat beef, you can limit your risk by avoiding the foods that are most likely to carry Mad Cow Disease: brains and processed beef products that may contain nervous-system tissue, such as hamburgers, hot dogs, and sausage. Beef labeled "organic" or "biodynamic" carries the least risk; inspections confirm that these cattle are not fed animal remains.

"A 2001 study . . . estimated that the number [of cases of mad cow disease] will probably top out at about 200."

Mad Cow Disease Is Not a Serious Threat

Michael Fumento

The American public and media recognize that bovine spongiform encephalopathy, or mad cow disease, does not pose a serious risk, Michael Fumento contends in the following viewpoint. He asserts that rather than frighten their readers with another exaggerated health scare, journalists have realized that there is no evidence that American consumers are at risk of eating tainted meat and contracting the deadly brain disease. Fumento concludes that Americans have no reason to fear the nation's meat supply. Fumento is a syndicated health and science columnist.

As you read, consider the following questions:

1. According to a survey cited by the author, what percentage of respondents thought the coverage of mad cow disease was "negatively biased?"

2. How many British cows have been infected by the prions associated with mad cow disease, according to Fumento?

Michael Fumento, "Not Having a Cow," *The Washington National Post Weekly Edition*, January 26, 2004, p. 23. Reproduced by permission of the author.

3. Why does Fumento believe media scares will continue to occur?

Remember those Wendy's commercials from 20 years ago? The ones where the granny would go into competing fast food restaurants, examine the hamburgers and obnoxiously demand, "Where's the beef?" I'm reminded, of those ads as I watch the media and public reaction to the news that mad cow disease has slipped over the border into the United States. My question is: "Where's the beef . . . hysteria?"

The announcement of mad cow disease is the sort of health scare that would normally have us fear-sensitized Americans reacting in a panic. So why aren't we out protesting hamburger restaurants or making like the French and dumping manure in McDonald's parking lots? We're not lynching cattlemen, tossing the beef from our freezers or converting en masse to vegetarianism. Last I heard, the singer Meat Loaf had yet to change his name to Tofu Burger.

For some reason, we're not stampeding down the fear trail over the (exceedingly slim) possibility that deadly prions could one day turn our brains into mush. This is notwithstanding the valiant efforts of "organic beef" and vegetarian groups, the Center for Science in the Public Interest (CSPI), animal rights activists and even most of the Democratic presidential candidates to scare the cow droppings out of us.

A Rational Response

"Consumer protection has certainly fallen short," declared CSPI in blasting the Agriculture Department. "Making meat 'safe' is not a realistic or attainable goal," declared meat-substitute producer Gardenburger on its Web site. And to Democratic hopeful Howard Dean, the mad cow case "raises serious concerns about the ability of this administration to protect the safety of our nation's food supply." Nevertheless, beef continues to be what's for dinner. We're still buying it—

and not the panic. This time, at least. The reasons have to do both with the specific nature of this case and with Americans' long-standing love affair with the hamburger, or a juicy red steak.

First, irrational as it seems, the media, after an initial flurry of the usual screaming headlines, are for once handling a scare story rationally. While keeping us informed of developments, they've generally refrained from the hype and horror that typify coverage of most health scares. In fact, there may be more accusations of media-motivated panic than there are media actually motivating panic. "When it comes to the safety of our food, media hysteria will be inversely proportional to actual risks," wrote one food writer, adding, "The mania surrounding mad cow is already proving this point."

But it isn't. While surveys consistently show that Americans believe the media to be heavily biased generally and biased toward sensationalism in particular, a Food Marketing Institute survey reported on Jan. 12 [2004] that only 22 percent of respondents considered the mad cow coverage "negatively biased." A Gallup Poll taken even before the reassuring news that the sick heifer was from Canada, where mad cow disease was already known to exist, showed that 55 percent of Americans had heard a "great deal" about mad cow disease in general, while another 33 percent said they'd heard a "moderate" amount. But those who had heard more were no more concerned than those who'd heard less. Overall, only 6 percent labeled the event "a crisis."

Just brave talk? No. Shares of stock in restaurant chains that rely heavily on beef sales, such as McDonald's Corp. and RARE Hospitality International, the owner of LongHorn Steakhouse, dipped initially but have since recovered. Jack in the Box's stock is doing considerably better than before the news hit. Meanwhile, though Gardenburger's stock more than doubled immediately after the announcement, it is now settling back to its earlier, pre-announcement levels.

Not a Major Epidemic

Why are the media and public still calmly chewing their cud? The disease itself is one mean mother. Properly called bovine spongiform encephalopathy (BSE) in the cow, it's labeled variant Creutzfeld-Jakob Disease (vCJD) when transferred to humans. The "spongiform" in "BSE" describes what it does to brains—theirs and ours. It's invariably fatal, with insanity as its hallmark. It also takes years to show up, meaning something you ate back in 1995 could strike you down next year. Are these not the ingredients for a media fright-fest?

Part of the explanation for the paucity of panic, though probably only a minor one, may be that there's no cause for it—and even the media know this. Because BSE was found in only one cow and authorities attempted to recall all of its meat, it's possible that nobody has taken a single bite from it. There's also no evidence that the prion proteins thought to cause the disease inhabit muscle; rather, they stay in the central nervous system. This would mean that whole cuts are off the hook, and that only parts that Americans generally consider disgusting, such as brains, eyeballs, tonsils and intestines, are potentially dangerous.

Watching the British over the last decade may also have helped us keep our heads level. Since the disease was first detected in herds in 1985–86, nearly 200,000 British cows have been discovered to be infected with the prions, and millions have been slaughtered because of possible infection. The United Kingdom's top BSE official said in 1996 that as many as half a million Britons would die from the bad beef, while an estimate in the *British Food Journal* a year earlier pegged potential deaths at as many as 10 million.

In fact, Britain's vCJD epidemic peaked in 1997, and fewer than 150 cases have been reported to date. A 2001 study in *Science* magazine estimated that the number will probably top out at about 200. All of this has caused a minor epidemic of

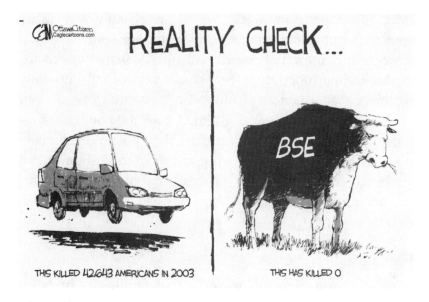

"Reality Check," cartoon by Cam Cardow. *Ottawa Citizen*, Caglecartoons.com. Reproduced by Cagle Cartoons, Inc.

red faces. And having been reported in the American media, the British example can't be ignored.

Other Health Scares

Still, a lack of cause for panic has hardly gotten in the way of our pitching other national hysterical fits. For several months [in 2003], you could hardly read even the sports section of a paper without coming across a story about SARS [Severe Acute Respiratory Syndrome]. Headlines like "Contagion of Fear Infects Americans" became self-fulfilling prophecies, while the *New York Times* and *Washington Post* between them ran more than 850 articles on the disease. Yet by the time most Americans even learned about SARS, it was already clear that it was a joke compared to the flu, which kills an average of 36,000 Americans a year. Ultimately, about 27 Americans contracted SARS, and none of them died.

Nor can the muted mad cow reaction be the result of Americans' finally developing immunity to what's commonly called "the scare of the week." We do tire of individual scares, even ones with some validity, such as the constantly changing colors of the Homeland Security Advisory System. But becoming blasé about one fear doesn't confer generalized immunity any more than a rabies vaccine will protect you from measles.

Even if we were becoming inured, how the populace is reacting or might react doesn't necessarily influence media coverage. The "farmed salmon will give you cancer" scare of two weeks ago got more than its share of irresponsible articles, although there's no evidence that it has had any effect on fish eaters.

Feeling Safe

A more reasonable explanation is that familiarity breeds a sense of safety. Beef is familiar. It's still our favorite meat. Americans eat more than 64 pounds per person per year (chicken is its closest competitor, at 53 pounds a year). Cattle-raising is part of the American culture. Maybe our love affair with beef is tied into our romance with the range, and the image of cowboys herding cattle across the plains. Can you think of any movies that feature free-range chicken farmers or pork producers as heroes? Then, too, the mad cow news hit at the same time that beef sales were sizzling due to the low-carbohydrate diet fad—maybe all those determined dieters weren't about to give up their steak minus potatoes.

Yes, beef was implicated in the Jack in the Box *E. coli* scare of 1993. But in that case, hundreds became violently ill; there were several deaths, and the primary victims were children. "Having children in the picture changes everything," says Christine Bruhn, a consumer food marketing specialist at the University of California at Davis.

There are other influential factors as well. One is "could it happen to you?" says David Ropeik, director of risk communication at the Harvard Center for Risk Analysis. It's reassuring that as far as we know, no American has contracted vCJD from American beef. Even with SARS, there were still those 29 victims. "With the anthrax [letters] scare, we all get the mail so there was panic," says Ropeik. "With the cow, people initially associated it only with Washington state, and only later with a total of eight states."

Media Scares Will Continue

Another factor, according to Ropeik, is that the media, especially TV, crave visuals. Yet TV news couldn't do much more than keep showing that one clip of a poor stumbling cow. They did also zero in on a human victim in Florida, but couldn't avoid explaining that she became infected while living in Britain. Even those images show her lying apparently comfortably in bed with no tubes or life support machines. Hospital tubes scare us.

Ropeik gives journalists a "B" on the mad cow issue "instead of a D minus," which he says is what they usually deserve on their coverage of potential health scares. I agree with that. But do I think that the mad cow (non)reaction is the start of a welcome and overdue trend? Not likely. The anti-fear factors I've described are particular to this case, making the lack of hysteria a pleasant but not prophetic exception.

As much as the public complains about media scares, they will continue to occur. Why? Because fear sells. Whether we admit it or not, we love the thrill these scares give us, probably because in most cases—as in watching a horror movie or riding a heart-stopping roller coaster—we know the threat they project is almost certainly a phantom menace.

| "The possible risks of eating plants with
| a few new genes are miniscule."

Genetically Modified Foods Are Safe

Gregory E. Pence

Genetically modified foods are safer to eat than are traditional foods, Gregory E. Pence claims in the following viewpoint. He argues that unlike processed foods, red meat, and poultry, genetically modified foods undergo numerous tests to ensure that they are safe to consume. In addition, he maintains that the likelihood that these new foods will contain allergens is slim. Pence is the author of Designer Food, *the source of this viewpoint.*

As you read, consider the following questions:

1. According to Pence, Monsanto subjected its Roundup Ready soybeans to how many analyses?
2. What two processes ensure that Americans are not exposed to allergens, as explained by the author?
3. How would the author relabel "genetically engineered" food?

Genetically engineered bovine growth hormone (rBGH) contains little possibility of infection with contaminated prions, viruses, or bacteria, unlike "naturally derived" BGH.

Gregory E. Pence, *Designer Food: Mutant Harvest or Breadbasket of the World?*, Lanham, MD: Rowman & Littlefield, 2002. Copyright © 2002 by Rowman & Littlefield Publishers, Inc. Reproduced by permission.

Similarly, genetically modified Chymosin, an enzyme that helps milk co-agulate in the production of cheese, used to be obtained from the stomachs of calves. Like Factor 8 clotting factor or rBGH, cloned chymosin is safer than the traditional form and allows moral vegetarians to feel good about eating cheese.

Extensive Tests

A second argument in favor of safety is that genetically altered crops are extensively tested, whereas new, crossbred variations of traditional crops are not. For example, [agricultural company] Monsanto subjected Roundup Ready soybeans to eighteen hundred analyses comparing the new soybeans to traditional ones for hundreds of substances and effects, including proteins and fatty acids. Monsanto concluded that the two kinds of soybeans did not differ in any way.

To prove safety to people, Monsanto fed high dosages of the enzyme made by the new soybeans to rats, chickens, and cows, with effects on animals identical to those produced by traditional soybeans. After human tests, the FDA [Food and Drug Administration] also found that enzymes of both new and old soybeans digest in human stomachs within fifteen seconds.

"We know more about the safety of Roundup soybeans than almost anything else we eat," said Anthony Trewavas, a professor at the University of Edinburgh [in Scotland]. Plant biochemists have a lot of experience with proteins and their tests show that Roundup Ready soybeans do not create dangerous new chemicals but create the same kind of proteins as traditional soybeans. Trewavas also points out that traditional crops haven't been tested at all, even though most such plants produce natural toxins and even though some new varieties of potato and celery created by Mendelian[1] methods have made people sick.

1. Referring to nineteenth-century monk and botanist Gregor Mendel, who developed the theory of genetics.

This is certainly worth emphasizing. Most people probably eat processed foods, such as fast foods and artificial creamers, that have received far less testing than Roundup soybeans. They also try new foods and spices in exotic restaurants (Ethiopian, Indonesian, Iranian), yet most such foods and spices have not been as extensively tested as GM [genetically modified] veggies.

Also, we have to trust someone, sometime. I see people ordering organic foods in a local restaurant but ordering Diet Cokes. Well, Diet Cokes contain saccharine, and the same scientists they distrust about GM food certified saccharine as safe after tests in rats. You can't pick and choose when you trust scientific results. . . .

Safer than Meat

Although this [viewpoint] is not an exposé of the meat industry, we must have some base of comparison if critics are going to say that a tomato with a few new genes out of thirty thousand might be unsafe. Compared to the dangers we face daily from eating beef, pork, and chicken, slightly changed vegetables seem hardly dangerous at all. The inherent dangers in our large, almost global, meat system create many risks from eating meat and, next to such risks, eating genetically modified plants seems just plain safe. . . .

I conclude that the risks from genetically modified fruits and vegetables are miniscule. Especially since these fruits and vegetables have been subjected to more thorough testing and monitoring than any new food in American history, they are very safe. No one has been harmed to date from eating genetically modified food, a claim that cannot be made about food produced by the meat industry. . . .

A Very Slight Danger

Dangers resulting from transfers of genes to plants, which in turn create unknown proteins that will produce allergic reac-

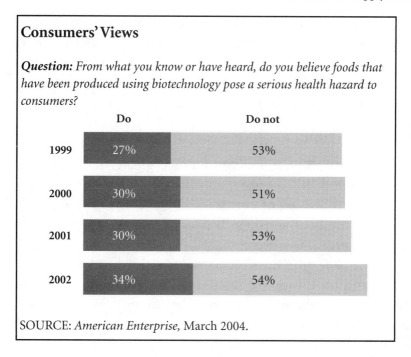

Consumers' Views

Question: From what you know or have heard, do you believe foods that have been produced using biotechnology pose a serious health hazard to consumers?

	Do	Do not
1999	27%	53%
2000	30%	51%
2001	30%	53%
2002	34%	54%

SOURCE: *American Enterprise,* March 2004.

tions in humans, seem slight. We know the major proteins that create allergic reactions in humans and can test for them. Already the FDA, manufacturers, and food processors agree that food containing proteins that are known allergens must be clearly labeled as such. Indeed, such GM foods have not yet even been created, much less labeled and sold, and probably will not be.

Two processes in America work to ensure little exposure of consumers to old or new allergens. First, food companies and the FDA, USDA [U.S. Department of Agriculture], and other federal agencies test novel foods for allergenicity. Precisely because this process of review worked, the soybean with the gene for Brazil nuts was not brought to market. Naturalists cannot legitimately cite a success of regulation as a reason why regulation is insufficient.

Second, real dangers of creating allergens carry risks of lawsuits, at least in America. Allergic reactions can be severe, sometimes resulting in anaphylactic shock and death. What food manufacturer will voluntarily introduce any allergen into his food, especially by stealth, when potential victims could sue him? Given popular fears about the term "genetic" and its conjunction with food, this would be stupid.

GM Food Presents a Minimal Risk

North American consumers face much greater dangers from the slaughtering, processing, and distribution of meat, pork, and chicken. As recent events in England have shown with mad cow and hoof-and-mouth diseases, the meat system is far more vulnerable to disease.

Along the same lines, genetically purified agents such as rBGH and chymosin are safer than natural, bovine-derived substances because infectious microbes cannot easily contaminate the cloned line. In these cases, "genetically engineered" food is really "genetically purified" food.

Overall, compared to what we tolerate in eating meat from an impersonal, centralized, industrial system, the possible risks of eating plants with a few new genes are miniscule.

"There is no scientific basis at this time for saying that [genetically modified] foods are problem free."

Genetically Modified Foods Are Not Safe

Martha Herbert

In the following viewpoint Martha Herbert argues that geneti-cally engineered food poses serious health risks. According to Herbert, these altered foods can contain new allergens, toxic lev-els of proteins, or antibiotic-resistant organisms. She further maintains that these foods are not adequately tested or labeled, which makes tracking the potential problems more difficult. She concludes that farmers should avoid the dangers associated with biotechnology and adopt less risky methods to improve their crops. Herbert is a pediatric neurologist at Harvard Medical School.

As you read, consider the following questions:

1. As explained by Herbert, what is the first step that must be taken when genetically engineering food?
2. What did a 1999 lawsuit against the FDA find, according to the author?
3. In the author's view, how are biological pollutants differ-ent than chemical toxins?

Martha Herbert, "What Is Genetically Modified Food (And Why Should You Care?)," *EarthSave Magazine*, Spring 2002, pp. 12-15. Copyright © 2002 EarthSave. Repro-duced by permission.

All living things contain genes. Genes contain information that helps shape how each living thing works. In genetic engineering, new genes are added that come from a different kind of living thing. These new genes confer certain desired characteristics, such as resistance to frost or to pesticides. The goal is to give these new characteristics to a living thing that couldn't do those things before.

What are genes?

Genes are strings of chemicals, called "nucleic acids," in DNA. The nucleic acids are like letters in an alphabet. Three of these letters in a row makes a little "code" and the code stands for a specific amino acid.

Amino acids are the building blocks of proteins. There are about two dozen of them. Proteins are the building blocks of living organisms. Proteins form the structures of living things, and form the enzymes living things use to carry out the chemical reactions they need to stay alive.

The order of the "nucleic acids" in DNA underlies the order of amino acids in proteins. And the order of amino acids in a [protein] affects what the protein will do. Your body contains a million or more different kinds of proteins, each with different jobs.

The Uniqueness of Genetic Engineering

Is genetic engineering different from other forms of breeding?

Yes, in two ways:

1. Before genetic engineering, plants and animals could only share genes through reproduction within their own species. With genetic engineering, genes from completely unrelated organisms can be introduced into our food supply. For example, moth or bacteria or fish genes can be engineered into plants. The most widely grown type of genetically engineered soybean, Monsanto's herbicide-resistant "Round Up Ready" soybean, contains genes from bacteria (Agrobacterium sp.), cauliflower virus, and

petunia. In experiments, technicians at the University of Illinois have inserted a cow gene into soybeans in order to alter a protein in the soy plant. This was field tested in 1998-1999.

2. Foreign genes are not welcomed by plants and animals. Therefore powerful techniques have to be used to force the plant or animal to take up the foreign genes.

Food and Genetic Engineering

How is genetic engineering of food done?

1. First the engineers try to get the outside gene in: The natural defenses of plants or animals against foreign genes need to be overcome. There are two main ways of doing this: the "gene gun" and the "viral vector." The "gene gun" shoots the gene into the recipient plant or animal. The "viral vector" infects it with the foreign gene.

2. Next, the engineers have to make sure the gene actually got in: Only about one in 10,000 attempts to introduce foreign genes actually works. Therefore, attached to the foreign gene is another gene, an "antibiotic resistance marker gene." If cells from the organism are grown in a dish containing that antibiotic, and they don't die, this means that the gene "got in."

3. Finally, the engineers have to make sure the gene actually gets used: The organism that received the foreign gene may ignore the gene. Therefore, a "promoter" is included with the gene to make sure the gene becomes active.

They say that genetic engineering is more precise than traditional breeding. Is that true?

No. Although genetic engineers know what gene they are putting in, they currently have no control over where it lands in the recipient organism's genome—and the position can make a lot of difference. It can land in the middle of another

"Genetically Altered Soup," cartoon by Simanca. Cagle Cartoons, Inc./Espanol. Reproduced by permission of Cagle Cartoons, Inc.

gene and disrupt that gene's function. Or, the "promoter" can increase the activity of other genes that normally would be silent. Genetic engineers have no control over these effects.

Also, in order to get a genetically engineered plant good enough to market, there have to be hundreds or thousands of failures, when genes get in but the plants or animals don't do very well, when they get sick from the genetically engineered changes.

The Risks of Genetic Engineering

Is genetic engineering safe?

Not necessarily. Genetic engineering has potential health risks. It also has the potential to harm the environment.

Health risks of genetically engineered foods:

1. Allergy or toxicity from new proteins in the food supply: Some of the genes used in genetic engineering were

never in the food supply before. There is no way to know ahead of time whether some people may become allergic to the proteins that result.

2. Allergy or toxicity from new ways of processing proteins: Plants and animals "process" proteins after they are produced by adding starch and other molecules that affect how the proteins function. Not all species do this in the same way. Different ways of processing proteins can lead to changes in function or changes in potential for allergy.

3. Allergy or toxicity or altered nutritional value from changing the way an organism functions: Genetic engineering can change the metabolism of a plant or animal. Proteins may be produced in increased quantities. Proteins that in small quantities were safe may now even exceed toxic levels. New proteins may be produced that were not produced before.

4. Antibiotic resistance genes may transfer into intestinal bacteria or other organisms and contribute to our growing public health problem of antibiotic-resistant organisms. Diseases that once could be treated by existing antibiotics may now become resistant to treatment.

A Lack of Monitoring

Aren't these foods being tested?

Actually, not much. The U.S. regulatory agencies ... rely on tests done by the companies that make these genetically engineered products. There are lots of questions that in-house testing doesn't ask. In particular, there is little to no screening for unexpected changes. No independent testing is required.

Aren't there safety standards for genetically engineered foods?

Genetically engineered foods were declared in 1992 to be "substantially equivalent" to traditional foods and therefore there is no requirement for testing. There was no scientific basis for this declaration and it is now being legally challenged. Clearly, foods that contain and were produced with viral promoters, pathogenic bacteria, and antibiotic resistant marker genes are NOT substantially equivalent to conventionally bred foods. In fact, in 1999, a major lawsuit against the FDA [Food and Drug Administration] uncovered documents showing that the FDA's own scientists had concluded that genetically engineered foods pose unique safety hazards and had recommended that each one should be subjected to rigorous, case-by-case safety testing. These safety warnings by the FDA's best scientists were ignored and then covered up by FDA bureaucrats. Regulatory standards for testing were designed before genetic engineering existed and have not been revised.

Isn't there health monitoring for effects of genetically engineered foods?

No. Some effects may be dramatic, as in severe toxic reactions. Effects will tend to be milder, however, and more long-term, as well as difficult to distinguish from problems caused by other things. No tests are available for allergies to these substances, so who is to say whether diarrhea, runny noses, headaches, or other signs of possible mild food allergy are coming from genetically engineered food or from the many other things we are exposed to every day? Tracing health problems to genetically engineered foods is almost impossible right now, because these foods are not labeled and there is no way to keep track of them. So there is no scientific basis at this time for saying that these foods are problem free. . . .

Why are corporations genetically engineering our food?

The biotechnology industry has invested many billions of dollars in genetic engineering and they want to make back their investment. They also hope to control all the levels of food production, from seeds and fertilizers to food processing and supermarkets. . . .

Biotechnology Is Not the Answer

If you're against biotech, then aren't you against science?

Actually there are a lot of smart, sophisticated alternatives to genetic engineering. In fact, genetic engineers tend to know very little about ecology or even about farming. Organic farming, sustainable agriculture and agro-ecology require more knowledge of plants, animals, insects and soil. These high-intelligence, low-technology, low-chemical approaches work with nature instead of biotech's approach of forcing nature to do things it wouldn't ordinarily do. They can work better, and without the risks of genetic engineering. But they don't get many research dollars because they can't be patented and they aren't a good source of profit for corporations.

The truth is that biotechnology is not cutting-edge science.

Can biotech change the world?

Yes—but perhaps not in ways we'd like to see. If we want to change the world for the better, we should probably look elsewhere. Releasing genetically engineered plants, animals and even bacteria into the environment is a form of biological pollution. Like chemical toxins, you cannot call them back. But unlike chemicals, biological pollutants can multiply and spread and interbreed, and change the balance of nature on our planet. If there are better ways to solve our food problems, why should we take this path?

| "More than 50 years of research have demonstrated that irradiating food can safely and effectively reduce illness from food-borne pathogens." |

Irradiation Makes Food Safer

Robin Brett Parnes, William C. Idell, Audrey L. Anastasia Kanik, and Alice H. Lichtenstein

In the following viewpoint Robin Brett Parnes, William C. Idell, Audrey L. Anastasia Kanik, and Alice H. Lichtenstein contend that exposing foods to gamma rays and X-rays, a process known as irradiation, improves food safety. They argue that irradiation offers benefits such as eliminating pathogens that lead to food-borne illness, decontaminating and sterilizing foods, and reducing the amount of bacteria in meat, poultry, and fish. According to the authors, more foods should be irradiated in order to ensure that America's food supply remains safe. Barnes is a writer and editor for HealthGate Data, Idell is a former graduate student at Tufts University in Boston, Kanik is a lecturer on nutrition and food safety, and Lichtenstein is a professor of nutrition science and policy at Tufts University.

As you read, consider the following questions:

1. How many people were hospitalized in 1999 as a result of food-borne illnesses, according to the authors?

2. As explained by the authors, how is sterilized food useful?

Nutrition Today, vol. 38, September-October 2003, pp. 174-185. Copyright © 2003 by Lippincott Williams & Wilkins. All rights reserved. Reproduced by permission.

3. According to a report cited by the authors, how many pounds of food products are irradiated in the United States each year?

Prevention of disease is a core public health mission. Food-borne illness is a major source of preventable morbidity and mortality. The Centers for Disease Control and Prevention (CDC) estimates that in 1999 food-borne illness caused 76 million illnesses, 325,000 hospitalizations, and 5,200 deaths in the United States. Between 1990 and 1999, nearly 300 outbreaks of food-borne illness occurred in schools, affecting approximately 16,000 children. Among all illnesses attributable to food-borne transmission, 30% are caused by bacteria, 67% by viruses, and 3% by parasites. Of the deaths attributable to food-borne illness, bacteria accounted for 72%, parasites 21%, and viruses 7%. Six pathogens have been identified as being responsible for more than 90% of the estimated food-related deaths: Salmonella (31%), Listeria (28%), Toxoplasma (21%), Norwalk-like viruses (7%), Campylobacter (5%), and Escherichia coli 0157:H7 (3%). Overall, the federal government spends approximately $1 billion on food safety measures. In addition, the Economic Research Service (ERS) of the US Department of Agriculture (USDA) estimates that through incurred medical costs, productivity losses, and premature deaths, food-borne illness costs the United States between $7 billion and $37 billion per year.

More than 50 years of research have demonstrated that irradiating food can safely and effectively reduce illness from food-borne pathogens. It can also extend the shelf life of foods by delaying ripening, inhibiting spoilage, and minimizing contamination. To a large extent, these potential benefits have yet to be realized in the United States because of the slow acceptance of this technology.

The food industry has been reluctant to sell irradiated foods because of a perception that consumers are unwilling to buy products associated with radiation. Unfortunately, little hard data are available to gauge potential consumer acceptance in the 21st century. Nevertheless, to date, 52 countries have given approval for irradiation of more than 100 food products.

The Development of Irradiation

Food irradiation uses ionizing radiation to extend the shelf life and increase the safety of several foods. Ionizing radiation is a form of electromagnetic radiation that contains adequate energy to dislodge electrons from the electron cloud surrounding individual atoms and molecules. The removal of electrons creates highly charged reactive products known as ions. The sources of ionizing radiation used in food irradiation are gamma rays, X-rays, and high-energy electron beams.

Interest in food irradiation dates back 100 years. After the discovery of X-rays by W.K. Roentgen in 1895 and the discovery of radioactive substances by H. Becquerel in 1896, much research was conducted exploring the biologic effects of radiation. The first patents were issued for use of ionizing radiation to kill bacteria in foods in 1905. In 1921, scientists at the USDA reported that X-rays effectively killed Trichina cysts in pork meat, showing they could kill disease-causing organisms and halt food spoilage. In 1943, scientists at the Massachusetts Institute of Technology demonstrated that X-rays could be used to preserve ground beef. Scientists [Bernard] Proctor and [Samuel] Goldblith reported in 1951 that the medium in which microorganisms are irradiated is a factor in determining the correct dose of radiation for bacterial inactivation; enzymes are more resistant to ionizing radiation than are bacteria, and irradiation in the frozen state minimizes the development of off-flavor in milk and orange juice.

To establish the safety and effectiveness of the irradiation process, the US Army and the Atomic Energy Commission (now part of the US Department of Energy) formed the National Food Irradiation Program, which conducted a series of experiments with fruits, vegetables, dairy products, fish, and meats lasting from 1953 through 1980. Large-scale work on food irradiation began in earnest after World War II, when radioactive isotopes and electron accelerators became available. Between 1964 and 1968, the US Army and the Atomic Energy Commission petitioned the Food and Drug Administration (FDA) to approve the irradiation of several packaging materials. In 1972, National Aeronautics and Space Administration (NASA) adopted irradiation to sterilize food for astronauts. As recently as 1999, the USDA has amended its regulations to allow the irradiation of refrigerated and frozen uncooked meat, meat by-products, and certain food products to control food-borne pathogens and extend shelf life. Additionally, in 2000, the FDA's regulations were amended to permit the irradiation of fresh shell eggs to control Salmonella. . . .

Uses of Food Irradiation

Reducing microbial growth. An estimated hundreds of millions of people worldwide suffer from diseases caused by consuming contaminated food. Food irradiation can be used to effectively eliminate pathogens that cause food-borne illness. For example, doses between < 1 kGy and 3 kGy reduce or eliminate populations of food-borne pathogens on produce. Additionally, a 3-kGy dose can kill 99.9% of Salmonella in poultry and an even higher percentage of E. coli 0157:H7 in ground beef. One approach to interrupt the reproductive mechanism of the pathogenic microorganisms is to disrupt their DNA. The larger the organism, the smaller the doses of irradiation. . . .

Food irradiation can also be used to extend the shelf life and decrease losses resulting from spoilage of fresh fruits and vegetables, as well as meats, fish, and poultry. The ERS reports that, although it is not possible to determine an exact number, evidence suggests that losses of edible food (primarily from microbial growth and the presence of insects and mold) on

Performing a Disservice

By instituting a fear-mongering campaign against irradiated meat, [consumer advocacy organization] Public Citizen and those who support their cause are misinforming the public about the true nature of modern irradiation methods—which are really nothing more than electronic pasteurization. They also are doing a terrible disservice to the U.S. meat industry, which has made significant strides in its efforts to detect and eliminate harmful bacteria in meat products.

Kelly Lenz, Topeka Capital-Journal, *December 26, 2002.*

the farm, as well as between the farm and retail levels, can be "significant for certain commodities." Treatment of strawberries with a dose of 2 kGy to 3 kGy followed by refrigeration at 10°C can eliminate the Botrytis mold and effectively increase their shelf life for up to 14 days. For meats and poultry, the predominant microbial spoilage organisms are the bacteria Pseudomonas and Achromobacter. A dose of 2.5 kGy can reduce many, but not all, of these bacteria, effectively doubling the shelf life of these products when stored at temperatures below 5°C. Fish and shellfish require doses of 0.75 kGy to 1.5 kGy for fresh products and 2 kGy to 5 kGy for frozen products. Studies indicate that these doses combined with storage temperatures below 3°C can extend the shelf life of fresh fish for 1 to 3 weeks and double the shelf life of frozen fish.

Inhibition of Sprouting

For many plant foods, inhibition of sprouting resulting from irradiation can increase their storage life. A radiation dose of up to 0.15 kGy can inhibit the sprouting of tubers, such as potatoes, yams, onions, garlic, and ginger, by inhibiting cell division within the food.

Making Foods Safer

Insect disinfestation. Contamination by insects is a problem with dried grains, cereals, coffee beans, and dried fruits, as well as fresh citrus fruits, mangoes, and papayas. Most insects can be rendered sterile with radiation doses between 0.05 kGy and 0.75 kGy. It has been suggested that imported fresh fruits and vegetables be treated with a dose of 0.15 kGy as a quarantine measure to help control for fruit flies.

Decontamination. Irradiation is a viable approach to treat spices, seasonings, fruits, and vegetables that can become heavily contaminated by pests because of poor environmental and processing conditions. The lack of heat in irradiation can preserve the flavor, color, and aromas of these products while effectively decreasing the microbial load. Spices can be irradiated at doses up to 30 kGy.

Delay ripening. Doses of 0.25 kGy to 0.35 kGy can suppress the ripening of bananas, mangoes, papayas, guava, and other tropical and subtropical fruits. Food irradiation causes little change in the "fresh" characteristics of foods, because the process does not raise the temperature of foods much, if at all, at the doses used.

Sterilization. Sterilization of foods can be achieved at doses of 10 kGy to 50 kGy. If packaged adequately, foods that are sterilized by irradiation can be stored for years without refrigeration, similar to canned (heat-sterilized) foods. Sterilized food is useful in hospitals for patients with severely impaired immune systems, such as patients with AIDS or patients undergoing chemotherapy. Sterilized irradiated foods are also currently being used at the International Space Station.

Environmental advantages. Food irradiation could replace chemical fumigants and use of vapor heat processes, resulting in a reduction or elimination of chemical residues in food and less harm to the environment. . . .

Making Irradiation More Popular

Although evidence indicates that irradiation is safe and effective and is endorsed worldwide by prominent scientific and health-related organizations, availability of irradiated food products in the United States has been limited. According to a report by the General Accounting Office (GAO) that was published in August 2000, an estimated 97 million pounds of food products are irradiated in the United States every year, which is only a small portion of the total amount of food consumed. Spices, herbs, and seasonings comprise the majority (98%) of food products that are irradiated. It has been speculated that food processors and retailers have kept the supply of irradiated foods low because they perceive that consumers are reluctant to buy irradiated foods and because of the high capital costs of irradiation equipment. As a result, healthcare and food service establishments, serving customers who are at risk of food-borne disease, remain the primary users of irradiated food.

Despite its numerous benefits, the food industry has been hesitant to fully use food irradiation technology because of perceived misgivings consumers have about radiation in general. Additionally, retail outlets carry only a limited number of irradiated products, because they fear negative attention from the few vocal public interest groups (namely, Public Citizen, Cancer Prevention Coalition, and Food and Water, Inc) opposed to food irradiation, who claim that it is used to mask unsanitary slaughtering and processing practices. However, food irradiation does not replace, but rather complements, proper food handling and GMPs by producers and processors. Meat and poultry establishments that use irradiation are required to meet sanitation and Hazard Analysis and Critical Control Point (HACCP) regulations. For the most part, consumers do not fully understand and have not thought much about food irradiation as a processing or food safety technology. Moreover, consumers trust our food supply and are willing to purchase irradiated foods. In fact, the few studies of consumer attitudes toward food irradiation that have been conducted show that, given information about the technology, half or more will choose irradiated foods. In a survey conducted in November 2001, 52% of the respondents said that because of the threat of bioterrorism, the government should require irradiation to help ensure a safe food supply.

The recently passed 2002 Farm Bill includes a provision directing the Secretary of Health and Human Services (HHS) to redefine pasteurization to include any process that HHS has approved to improve food safety. Irradiation is one of those processes. Consequently, companies may be able to use "cold pasteurized" or "electronic pasteurized" on products that have been irradiated, which, if implemented, could potentially allay consumer concerns about food irradiation. The Farm Bill also allows for schools participating in the school lunch program to purchase irradiated meat for students by the end of the year.

Although the US food supply is considered to be among the safest in the world, food-borne illness remains a serious public health problem. Increased use of food irradiation could provide an additional tool with which to reduce the occurrence of food-borne illness and costs associated with such outbreaks. Furthermore, it can increase the availability of a wider variety of foods to the consumer by extending shelf life of highly perishable foods. Theoretically, an initial capital investment to increase food irradiation capacity in the United States could be offset by decreased loss resulting from spoilage. Critical in this process would be adequate consumer education and strong government oversight. Regardless of changes that may be made to labeling requirements, food irradiation is an underused technology that could potentially play a major role within a comprehensive strategy to keep our food supply safe.

> *"Irradiation . . . cannot prevent con-
> tamination, nor protect food from fur-
> ther contamination after it has been
> treated."*

Irradiation Has Limited Benefits

Rose Marie Williams

*Although irradiation (exposing foods to gamma rays and X-rays)
can kill harmful bacteria, it is not wholly effective in making
America's food supply safer, Rose Marie Williams asserts in the
following viewpoint. She argues that irradiation does not offer
protection against mad cow disease, and notes that it cannot
protect food from posttreatment contamination. Williams further
opines that irradiation destroys valuable nutrients in foods and
poses health risks to workers in the irradiating facilities. Williams is a medical researcher and regular contributor to* Townsend
Letter for Doctors and Patients.

As you read, consider the following questions:

1. According to Williams, why does irradiation not protect
   against mad cow disease?
2. What does the author assert is the cheapest alternative
   to irradiation?

Rose Marie Williams, "Irradiated Food Controversy—Health Risks and Environmental
Issues," *Townsend Letter for Doctors and Patients*, November 2003. Copyright © 2003
The Townsend Letter Group. Reproduced by permission of the author.

3. According to the author, what carcinogen appears in a higher concentration in irradiated beef than in cooked beef?

The food and nuclear industries, backed by government support, are using recent outbreaks of meat poisoning as a rallying call to "mobilize public acceptance of large scale food irradiation." The Food and Drug Administration (FDA) already allows the irradiation of beef, pork, poultry, eggs, vegetables, fruit, flour, and spices, while the US Department of Agriculture (USDA) is advocating "the imminent irradiation of imported fruits and vegetables." Some supermarkets and fast food chains have recently begun to offer irradiated meat products, while irradiated spices have been a staple for several years.

A media campaign to win over consumer confidence is in full swing. Wegman Supermarkets have taken out full-page ads advising customers they can now cook juicy irradiated burgers "the way they like," and "without worrying about safety," implying that juicy (and rare) are now completely safe. A Minneapolis Dairy Queen poster advises customers to "Enjoy with Confidence!" while a pamphlet from the Sure Beam Company insists "You can't taste the difference."

Selling Irradiation

Researchers at *Consumer Reports* embarked on the largest analysis yet of tasting and testing 500 meat samples from 60 cities for bacterial content of irradiated and non-irradiated chicken and ground beef from retail outlets. They found bacteria levels in the irradiated, uncooked ground beef and skinless chicken tenders to be much lower than levels in non-irradiated meat, though not completely bacteria-free. Irradiation does not protect meat products indefinitely. Irradiated meats can be re-contaminated from improper handling.

Consumer Reports trained taste-testers noted a slight, but distinct, off-taste and smell in most of the irradiated beef and chicken sampled, "likening it to singed hair."

Cooking destroys more bacteria than does irradiation, and irradiated meats come with the same cooking instructions as regular meat. Higher prices and singed flavor hardly seem like desirable qualities, which is why the advertising campaign is going into high gear to convince consumers of the "safety" benefits. Several major food outlets already offer irradiated meat—Food Emporium, Giant Food, Publix, and Shop Rite, along with restaurant chains such as Dairy Queen and Embers America. Wal-Mart, the country's largest food retailer, is testing sales of irradiated meat in its Northeast stores before offering it nationwide. Irradiated meat is currently being sold in 40 other chain stores around the US including Albertsons, Giant Eagle, Harris Teeter, Schnuks and Tops. Dierberg's Markets in Missouri, and Raley's in California, Nevada, and New Mexico are considering it. If you shop there, you can let them know you don't want it. McDonald's, the world's largest fast-food chain, has indicated they are not using irradiated foods, and are not planning to do so.

The Irradiation Process

Irradiation exposes foods to ionizing radiation from Cobalt 60, Cesium 137, X-rays, or high-energy electron beams from machine sources capable of breaking chemical bonds. Also referred to as "ionizing radiation" it produces energy waves strong enough to dislodge electrons from atoms and molecules, converting them to electrically charged particles called ions. Ionizing radiation is often referred to as "cold pasteurization" and "irradiation pasteurization." Gamma rays produced from Cobalt, Cesium 137, and X-rays can penetrate food to much greater depths than electron beams, which are only able to penetrate a maximum of one inch for most foods, or three inches if irradiated from both sides. Electron beams

Low-Tech Alternatives

The CDC [Centers for Disease Control and Prevention] says 20 percent of foodborne outbreaks are caused simply by commercial food preparers' poor-hygiene, such as failing to wash hands before touching food. The Department of Agriculture reported eliminating 99.9 percent of E. coli O157:H7 in spiked beef samples with a low-tech step: spraying beef with lactic acid, a food preservative with antimicrobial properties, before grinding.

"It's better to take steps to avoid contaminating food to begin with than it is to try to clean it up afterwards," says Carol Tucker Foreman, director of the Food Policy Institute of the Consumer Federation of America and former assistant secretary of the USDA [U.S. Department of Agriculture]. "But I'm afraid it's human nature not to spend money to change the way animals are raised, or have a trained workforce in meatpacking plants, or upgrade facilities if they can just irradiate food at the end of the line."

Consumer Reports, *August 2003.*

are not produced from radioactive sources and have no radioactive waste, but do create ionizing changes in foods, similar to other forms of irradiation.

Ionizing radiation reduces the number of disease-causing organisms in food by disrupting their molecular structure and killing potentially harmful bacteria and parasites. However, when food is irradiated, some nutrients are destroyed and untested compounds, referred to as URPs (unique radiolytic products), may be created.

Irradiation of food has been found to inactivate several food-borne pathogens such as E. coli 0157:H7, Bacillus cereus, Clostridium botulinum, Listeria monocytogene, Salmonella,

Staphylococcus aureus, Campylobacter jejuini, Cyclospora, and Taxoplasma gondii. While capable of reducing the number of pathogens in foods, irradiation does not destroy all the dangerous organisms, nor does it prevent later contamination from improper handling or storage. Sure Beam of Sioux City, Iowa, the country's largest food irradiator, uses the new electron beam (e-beam), which generates a beam of accelerated electrons or X-rays approaching the speed of light. A company spokesperson indicated it is much safer because there are no radioactive components. Sure Beam was described as "environmentally friendly" since it also replaces the use of methyl bromide, a toxic chemical used in food preservation. More information about Sure Beam is available from their website: www.surebeam.com.

Problems with Electron Beams

Electron beam is a relatively new technology in the food irradiation industry, and while it does not use radioactive components, it is not completely danger-free. Critics cite two serious employee accidents. In 1991, ignoring safety warnings, a Maryland worker received a 5,000-rad dose from a 3-million electron-volt linear accelerator and lost four fingers. A 1992 mishap at a 15-million electron-volt linear accelerator in Hanoi resulted in the loss of a hand and several fingers to the facility's research director.

Food Technology Service, the nation's largest gamma-ray meat irradiator, claims the energy passes through food much as "a ray of light passes through a window." But this is no ordinary ray of light. It is a powerful ray—"1.5 kilo Grays is 15 million times the energy involved in a single chest X-ray, or 150 times the dose capable of killing an adult."

Irradiation damages the DNA of disease-causing bacteria, insects and parasites making them "inactive" and incapable of reproducing. The approved doses are not sufficient for eliminating all the bacteria in meat. To do that, much higher doses would be necessary and this would seriously affect the flavor of the meat. Irradiation offers no protection against mad-cow disease believed to be caused by prions, which contain no DNA.

The government is allowing ground beef contaminated with E. coli 0157:H7, ordinarily considered unlawful to sell, to be irradiated and then offered to consumers.

The Limitations of Irradiation

- Irradiation greatly reduces bacterial content in foods, but is considered less effective than proper cooking and improved sanitation practices.

- Irradiation would not protect against mad-cow disease, because prions contain no DNA. Prions are thought to be responsible for the disease.

- Irradiation destroys necessary nutrients while creating carcinogenic and mutagenic radiolytic products.

- Irradiation facilities pose further health risks to workers, communities, and the environment.

- Irradiation is only applicable for a limited number of foods. Fresh produce is a major carrier of food-borne disease. Since irradiation turns fresh produce mushy and unpalatable its application is greatly diminished.

Not all scientists and food authorities support irradiation, and even its strongest proponents acknowledge that irradiation is not the solution to bad sanitation and substandard practices. Irradiation may help control contamination after it occurs, but cannot prevent contamination, nor protect food from further contamination after it has been treated. . . .

Alternatives to Irradiation

Pre-slaughter and post-evisceration sanitation at meat packing plants can be highly effective for reducing carcass contamination. This is considered very cost effective, because testing pooled carcasses for E. coli 0157 and Salmonella is economical, practical and rapid. [Samuel] Epstein and [Wenonah] Hauter believe the expense of producing sanitary meat would be trivial compared to high costs of irradiation, and potential dangers of nuclear accidents using this technology, with all expenses being passed onto the American taxpayer. Anticipated international bans on the import of irradiated food from the US, and a decline of overseas tourists concerned about eating irradiated food will result in a huge loss of revenue.

Unfortunately, too many consumers are eager to embrace a quick fix for every problem. Government approval combined with industry assurances and the accompanying media blitz will give many consumers a false sense of security and further delay efforts to clean up food production at the source of contamination.

Ozone treatment, pulsed light and high-pressure treatment are additional food sanitation technologies under development which may provide benefits similar to irradiation, but without the potential hazards.

The cheapest, easiest, safest, and healthiest alternative is the one designed by Mother Nature, which is to feed beef animals hay for one week before slaughter. As Dr. Epstein [has] pointed out, replacing the unnatural starchy grain diet with hay for a few days greatly reduces bacterial contamination in beef animals, and the resulting food-borne illnesses.

Changes in Terminology

Fully aware of the importance of image and the suggestibility of words, industry has petitioned to weaken the labeling requirements for irradiated food by eliminating the word "irradiated," which admittedly would discourage many consumers. The Appropriations Committees for both the House and Senate, under pressure from industry, have agreed to eliminate the word "irradiated" in favor of "electronic pasteurization."

Not only are these comfort words for the American consumer, but they also signify the best of what technology has offered our modern way of life. Electricity suggests convenience, while pasteurization implies safety.

The term, "electronic pasteurization," was proposed by San Diego-based Titan Corporation, a major defense contractor. The highly expensive linear accelerator, "E-beam" technology "originally designed for President [Ronald] Reagan's 'Star Wars' shoots food with a stream of electrons traveling at the speed of light." The FDA's approved meat radiation dosage of 450,000 rads is approximately 150 million times greater than that of a chest X-ray. Epstein and Hauter believe it is misleading to label the process "electronic pasteurization," because it circumvents the consumer's fundamental right to know. The food irradiation industry is strongly criticized for choosing to sanitize the label and not sanitize practices at slaughter and packing plants, which would have a much greater impact on protecting public health.

Health and Environmental Risks

According to federal and world health officials, irradiated food is safe to eat. But not everyone is convinced. Irradiated food does not become radioactive, but some chemical by-products are created in the meat. This has prompted many researchers and the European Parliament to request further testing. Nutritious food is fundamental to maintaining health. Mainstream medicine is finally recognizing this truth by hinting that heart disease and cancer may be reduced when more fresh vegetables, fruits, and whole grains are added to the diet. Irradiation destroys major micronutrients, particularly vitamins A, C, E, and the B-complex. The nutrient loss is further accelerated by cooking, resulting in "empty calorie" food. Irradiation has even been used to "clean up food unfit for human consumption, such as spoiled fish, by killing odorous contaminating bacteria."

Ionizing radiation produces highly reactive free radicals and peroxides from the unsaturated fats in meat which industry claims is the same as that produced from ordinary cooking. However, tests done in 1977 by the US Army showed major differences between volatile chemicals formed during irradiation or cooking meat. Carcinogenic benzene was found to be ten times higher in irradiated beef than in cooked beef. Other unique radiolytic chemical products implicated as carcinogens under certain conditions, were also identified.

These concerns caused FDA's 1980 Irradiation Food Committee to warn that safety testing should be based on concentrated extracts of irradiated foods, rather than on whole foods, to maximize the concentration of radiolytic products. "Until such fundamental studies are undertaken, there is little scientific basis for accepting industry's assurances of safety," warns Dr. Epstein.

Periodical Bibliography

Frank Ackerman and Lisa Heinzerling
"Balancing Lives," *Los Angeles Times*, February 25, 2004.

Jennifer Ackerman
"Food: How Safe? How Altered?" *National Geographic*, May 2002.

Jacqueline Adams
"Holy Cow! What Now? Mad Cow Disease Has Hit the U.S.: How Worried Should You Be?" *Science World*, March 8, 2004.

Clifton E. Anderson
"Biotech on the Farm," *Futurist*, September/October 2005.

Consumer Reports
"The Truth About Irradiated Meat," August 2003.

Carol Tucker Foreman
"Killing the 'Frankenfood' Monster," *American Enterprise*, March 2004.

T.A. Heppenheimer
"The Growth of Genetically Modified Foods," *Invention & Technology*, Summer 2003.

Issues and Controversies On File
"Genetically Modified Food Update," July 22, 2005.

Lancet
"How Safe Is GM Food?" October 26, 2002.

Debora MacKenzie
"American Nightmare," *New Scientist*, August 7, 2004.

Richard McGill Murphy
"Truth or Scare," *American Demographics*, March 2004.

Charles W. Schmidt
"Genetically Modified Foods: Breeding Uncertainty," *Environment Health Perspectives*, August 2005.

USA Today Magazine
"Attacks on Food Supply Unlikely to Succeed," April 2002.

OPPOSING
VIEWPOINTS®
SERIES

CHAPTER 2

How Should Farms Be Operated?

Chapter Preface

The produce sections of grocery stores are filled with foods from around the nation and world, with nearly all fruits and vegetables available year-round. Many Americans view this wealth of choices as a benefit. However, this view is disputed by advocates of local farming. They contend that keeping food production close to home is better for the environment, the local economy, and may even help guard against terrorism.

According to supporters of local farming, the global agricultural network exacts high environmental and economic costs. In an article for Oxfam America, Marika Alena McCauley points out that the average food item travels thirteen hundred miles before reaching a grocery store. She and others argue that transporting food this distance harms the environment because high amounts of fossil fuels are burned, which can lead to air pollution and possibly global warming. By contrast, she writes, "Food produced and consumed locally uses less fossil fuel for transportation and requires less material for packaging compared to mainstream food production." Moreover, McCauley states that only 10 percent of the money spent on food goes to the farmers; the remaining dollars are spent on marketing, transportation, and packaging. In contrast, advocates argue, when people buy local foods the profits do not go to distant food conglomerates but to the people who grow the food. Peter M. Rosset, in a policy brief for Food First/Institute for Food and Development Policy, asserts that local farming translates into stronger rural economies and empowers farmers by producing "more equitable economic opportunity for people in rural areas."

Local farming may also be the best way to guard against bioterrorism and ensure food safety, its supporters contend. Jennifer Wilkins, a food and society policy fellow at Cornell

University, writes that local farmers can protect against unsafe food because they do not rely on centralized food processors or import potentially tainted foods. She writes, "The combination of cheap food from overseas and the consolidation of domestic production compromises America's ability to feed itself. A food system in which control of the critical elements is concentrated in a few hands can and will fall victim to terrorism or accidents." Wilkins argues that the solution is to give farmers more control over food quality by establishing "community-based food systems that include many small farmers and a diversity of products."

Even taking into account the benefits of buying locally grown produce, it remains to be seen whether consumers will embrace it. Americans have grown used to having every imaginable fruit and vegetable available to them year-round. However, growing support for these farms illustrates increasing controversy over how farms are operated. The authors in the following chapter debate the best ways to run modern farms.

> *"Factory farming has no traditions, no rules, no codes of honor, no little decencies to spare for a fellow creature."*

Animals Should Be Treated More Humanely on Factory Farms

Matthew Scully

Animals bred for meat are treated cruelly on most large American farms, Matthew Scully maintains in the following viewpoint. He contends that the conditions on these factory farms are inhumane, with the operators crowding animals in iron crates, mutilating them, and refusing to provide the sick with medical treatment. According to Scully, the owners and operators of these farms lack compassion and are only interested in profits. Scully is the author of Dominion: The Power of Man, the Suffering of Animals, and the Call to Mercy.

As you read, consider the following questions:

1. How did factory farms originate, according to Scully?
2. In the author's view, why is factory farming "a predatory enterprise?"
3. What is the logic of Judeo-Christian morality, according to the author?

Matthew Scully, "Fear Factories: The Case for Compassionate Conservatism—For Animals," *American Conservative*, May 23, 2005, Copyright © 2005 The American Conservative. Reproduced by permission.

A few years ago I began a book about cruelty to animals and about factory farming in particular, problems that had been in the back of my mind for a long while. At the time I viewed factory farming as one of the lesser problems facing humanity—a small wrong on the grand scale of good and evil but too casually overlooked and too glibly excused.

This view changed as I acquainted myself with the details and saw a few typical farms up close. By the time I finished the book, I had come to view the abuses of industrial farming as a serious moral problem, a truly rotten business for good reason passed over in polite conversation. Little wrongs, when left unattended, can grow and spread to become grave wrongs, and precisely this had happened on our factory farms. . . .

Making Excuses for Mistreating Animals

Where animals are concerned, there is no practice or industry so low that someone, somewhere, cannot produce a high-sounding reason for it. The sorriest little miscreant who shoots an elephant, lying in wait by the water hole in some canned-hunting operation, is just "harvesting resources," doing his bit for "conservation." The swarms of government-subsidized Canadian seal hunters slaughtering tens of thousands of new-born pups—hacking to death these unoffending creatures, even in sight of their mothers—offer themselves as the brave and independent bearers of tradition. With the same sanctimony and deep dishonesty, factory-farm corporations like Smithfield Foods, ConAgra, and Tyson Foods still cling to countrified brand names for their labels—Clear Run Farms, Murphy Family Farms, Happy Valley—to convince us and no doubt themselves, too, that they are engaged in something essential, wholesome, and honorable.

Yet when corporate farmers need barbed wire around their Family Farms and Happy Valleys and laws to prohibit outsiders from taking photographs (as is the case in two states) and still other laws to exempt farm animals from the definition of "animals" as covered in federal and state cruelty statutes, something is amiss. And if conservatives do nothing else about any other animal issue, we should attend at least to the factory farms, where the suffering is immense and we are all asked to be complicit. If we are going to have our meats and other animal products, there are natural costs to obtaining them, defined by the duties of animal husbandry and of veterinary ethics. Factory farming came about when resourceful men figured out ways of getting around those natural costs, applying new technologies to raise animals in conditions that would otherwise kill them by deprivation and disease. With no laws to stop it, moral concern surrendered entirely to economic calculation, leaving no limit to the punishments that factory farmers could inflict to keep costs down and profits up. Corporate farmers hardly speak anymore of "raising" animals, with the modicum of personal care that word implies. Animals are "grown" now, like so many crops. Barns somewhere along the way became "intensive confinement facilities" and the inhabitants mere "production units."

The result is a world in which billions of birds, cows, pigs, and other creatures are locked away, enduring miseries they do not deserve, for our convenience and pleasure. We belittle the activists with their radical agenda, scarcely noticing the radical cruelty they seek to redress. At the Smithfield mass-confinement hog farms I toured in North Carolina, the visitor is greeted by a bedlam of squealing, chain rattling, and horrible roaring. To maximize the use of space and minimize the need for care, the creatures are encased row after row, 400 to 500 pound mammals trapped without relief inside iron crates seven feet long and 22 inches wide. They chew maniacally on bars and chains, as foraging animals will do when denied straw, or engage in stereotypical nest-building with the straw that isn't there, or else just lie there like broken beings. The spirit of the place would be familiar to police who raided that Tennessee puppy-mill run by Stanley and Judy Johnson, only

An International Problem

If [Upton Sinclair's novel] *The Jungle* were written today, it might not be set in the American Midwest. Developing nations like the Philippines are becoming the centers of large-scale livestock production and processing to feed the world's growing appetite for cheap meat and other animal products. Ironically, the situations Sinclair exposed a century ago, including hazardous working conditions, unsanitary processing methods, and environmental contamination, still exist. Some have become even worse. As environmental regulations in the European Union and the U.S. become stronger, large agribusinesses are moving their operations to nations with less stringent enforcement of environmental laws.

These intensive processing methods are spreading all over the globe, from Canada to Mexico, from India to the former USSR, and most rapidly throughout Asia. Wherever they crop up, they create a web of related food safety, animal welfare, and environmental concerns.

Danielle Nierenberg, USA Today Magazine, *January 2004.*

instead of 350 tortured animals, millions—and the law prohibits none of it.

Afflicted Animals

Efforts to outlaw the gestation crate have been dismissed by various conservative critics as "silly," "comical," "ridiculous." It doesn't seem that way up close. The smallest scraps of human charity—a bit of maternal care, room to roam outdoors, straw to lie on—have long since been taken away as costly luxuries, and so the pigs know the feel only of concrete and metal. They lie covered in their own urine and excrement, with broken legs from trying to escape or just to turn, covered with festering sores, tumors, ulcers, lesions, or what my guide shrugged off as the routine "pus pockets."

C.S. Lewis's description of animal pain—"begun by Satan's malice and perpetrated by man's desertion of his post" —has literal truth in our factory farms because they basically run themselves through the wonders of automation, and the owners are off in spacious corporate offices reviewing their spreadsheets. Rarely are the creatures' afflictions examined by a vet or even noticed by the migrant laborers charged with their care, unless of course some ailment threatens production— meaning who cares about a lousy ulcer or broken leg, as long as we're still getting the piglets? Kept alive in these conditions only by antibiotics, hormones, laxatives, and other additives mixed into their machine-fed swill, the sows leave their crates only to be driven or dragged into other crates, just as small, to bring forth their piglets. Then it's back to the gestation crate for another four months, and so on back and forth until after seven or eight pregnancies they finally expire from the punishment of it or else are culled with a club or bolt-gun.

As you can see at www.factoryfarming.com/gallery.htm, industrial livestock farming operates on an economy of scale, presupposing a steady attrition rate. The usual comforting rejoinder we hear—that it's in the interest of farmers to take good care of their animals—is false. Each day, in every confinement farm in America, you will find cull pens littered with dead or dying creatures discarded like trash.

For the piglets, it's a regimen of teeth cutting, tail docking (performed with pliers, to heighten the pain of tail chewing and so deter this natural response to mass confinement), and other mutilations. After five or six months trapped in one of the grim warehouses that now pass for barns, they're trucked off, 355,000 pigs every day in the life of America, for processing at a furious pace of thousands per hour by migrants who use earplugs to muffle the screams. All of these creatures, and billions more across the earth, go to their deaths knowing nothing of life, and nothing of man, except the foul, tortured existence of the factory farm, having never even been outdoors.

An Indecent Method

But not to worry, as a Smithfield Foods executive assured me, "They love it." It's all "for their own good." It is a voice conservatives should instantly recognize, as we do when it tells us that the fetus feels nothing. Everything about the picture shows bad faith, moral sloth, and endless excuse-making, all readily answered by conservative arguments. We are told "they're just pigs" or cows or chickens or whatever and that only urbanites worry about such things, estranged as they are from the realities of rural life. Actually, all of factory farming proceeds by a massive denial of reality—the reality that pigs and other animals are not just production units to be endlessly exploited but living creatures with natures and needs. The very modesty of those needs—their humble desires for straw, soil, sunshine—is the gravest indictment of the men who deny them.

Conservatives are supposed to revere tradition. Factory farming has no traditions, no rules, no codes of honor, no little decencies to spare for a fellow creature. The whole thing is an abandonment of rural values and a betrayal of honorable animal husbandry—to say nothing of veterinary medicine, with its sworn oath to "protect animal health" and to "relieve animal suffering." . . .

Economic Excuses

Factory farmers also assure us that all of this is an inevitable stage of industrial efficiency. Leave aside the obvious reply that we could all do a lot of things in life more efficiently if we didn't have to trouble ourselves with ethical restraints. Leave aside, too, the tens of billions of dollars in annual federal subsidies that have helped megafarms undermine small family farms and the decent communities that once surrounded them and to give us the illusion of cheap products. And never mind the collateral damage to land, water, and air that factory farms cause and the mere billions of dollars it costs taxpayers to clean up after them. Factory farming is a predatory enterprise, absorbing profit and externalizing costs, unnaturally propped up by political influence and government subsidies much as factory-farmed animals are unnaturally sustained by hormones and antibiotics.

Even if all the economic arguments were correct, conservatives usually aren't impressed by breathless talk of inevitable progress. I am asked sometimes how a conservative could possibly care about animal suffering in factory farms, but the question is premised on a liberal caricature of conservatism—the assumption that, for all of our fine talk about moral values, "compassionate conservatism" and the like, everything we really care about can be counted in dollars. In the case of factory farming, and the conservative's blithe tolerance of it, the caricature is too close to the truth.

Exactly how far are we all prepared to follow these industrial and technological advances before pausing to take stock of where things stand and where it is all tending? Very soon companies like Smithfield plan to have tens of millions of cloned animals in their factory farms. Other companies are at work genetically engineering chickens without feathers so that one day all poultry farmers might be spared the toil and cost of de-feathering their birds. For years, the many shills for our livestock industry employed in the "Animal Science" and "Meat Science" departments of rural universities (we used to call them Animal Husbandry departments) have been tampering with the genes of pigs and other animals to locate and expunge that part of their genetic makeup that makes them stressed in factory farm conditions—taking away the desire to protect themselves and to live. Instead of redesigning the factory farm to suit the animals, they are redesigning the animals to suit the factory farm.

Are there no boundaries of nature and elementary ethics that the conservative should be the first to see? The hubris of such projects is beyond belief, only more because of the foolish and frivolous goods to be gained—blood-free meats and the perfect pork chop.

No one who does not profit from them can look at our modern factory farms or frenzied slaughter plants or agricultural laboratories with their featherless chickens and fear-free pigs and think, "Yes, this is humanity at our finest—exactly as things should be." Devils charged with designing a farm could hardly have made it more severe. Least of all should we look for sanction in Judeo-Christian morality, whose whole logic is one of gracious condescension, of the proud learning to be humble, the higher serving the lower, and the strong protecting the weak.

> *"Farm animal experts have given the foodservice industry widespread credit for recent animal welfare initiatives."*

Animals Are Not Mistreated on Factory Farms

Amy Garber and James Peters

In the following viewpoint Amy Garber and James Peters argue that the treatment of animals on large farms has improved significantly over the past decade. They argue that companies such as McDonald's are taking the lead by requiring that their agricultural suppliers provide increased living space for animals and end the practice of debeaking chickens. Garber and Peters further argue that the food industry is working to develop a single system of guidelines to aid in monitoring conditions at America's large animal farms and slaughterhouses. Garber is the senior editor of Nation's Restaurant News, *and Peters is a writer for the publication.*

As you read, consider the following questions:

1. What tactics by People for the Ethical Treatment of Animals have been criticized by the National Restaurant Association, according to the authors?

2. According to Garber and Peters, how many eggs does McDonald's purchase each year?

Amy Garber and James Peters, "Latest Pet Project: Better Treatment for Animals: Industry Agencies Try to Create Protocol for Improving Living, Slaughtering Conditions," *Nation's Restaurant News*, September 22, 2003, pp. 108-110. Copyright © 2003 Nation's Restaurant News. Reprinted by permission of the publisher.

3. How does Wesley J. Smith, as quoted by the authors, say restaurants should defend themselves against PETA?

In its latest campaign against a fast-food behemoth, PETA, or People for the Ethical Treatment of Animals, has employed such heavy-handed tactics as creating a Web site that is filled with graphic images of animal abuse and even throwing fake blood on a CEO.

And when those maneuvers failed to produce the desired effect, PETA paid a visit to the city where the quick-service company is based. Several of the group's activists walked door-to-door to visit the foodservice executives' neighbors in an effort to make its case for stepped-up animal-handling guidelines. PETA representatives also made stops at local churches and restaurants, passing out leaflets, stickers and other literature.

Harsh Attacks

PETA makes no qualms about its relentless strategy of targeting major restaurant chains, explaining that such harsh tactics—which are intended to grab headlines and sway public opinion—bring about reform much more quickly than does lobbying on Capitol Hill.

"We can adversely affect the bottom line and stock price of public companies like McDonald's and KFC in a way that we don't have the money or the influence to change the USDA [U.S. Department of Agriculture] or the agriculture committees in the House and Senate," says Bruce Friedrich, PETA's vegan-outreach director. "They [members of Congress] tend to be unwilling to pass legislation that is not supported by animal agri-business. That is why we have focused on corporations that have customers to lose."

After initially attacking burger chains to improve practices in cattle slaughterhouses, PETA most recently focused on improving conditions for chickens. As a result, the group has targeted Yum! Brands Inc. and its KFC chain. Yum, based in Louisville, Ky., also owns Pizza Hut, Taco Bell, A&W, Long John Silver's and Pasta Bravo.

Campaigning Against KFC

[In 2003] a PETA activist threw fake blood on Yum's chairman and chief executive, David Novak, as he entered a co-branded KFC-A&W unit in Germany. While the group initially denied a role in the attack, it later claimed credit for it.

PETA mounted another attack in July [2003] when it slapped Yum and KFC with a lawsuit accusing the chicken chain of making misleading statements about its poultry welfare guidelines. After KFC removed from its Web sites information about its guidelines, PETA dropped the litigation, but it still plans to continue its anti-KFC campaign with a "world week of action" Sept. 28 through Oct. 4 [2003]. During that week PETA will hold demonstrations at KFC outlets "in all 50 states and in dozens of countries around the world," Friedrich says.

Seen as Terrorists

Nonetheless, farm animal experts have given the foodservice industry widespread credit for recent animal welfare initiatives. But PETA's aggressive strategy has become more than a thorn in the side for many restaurateurs, causing the National Restaurant Association to compare the group's approach to "terrorism."

Steve Grover, the NRA's [National Rifle Association] vice president of health, safety and regulatory affairs, explains that PETA has "picketed in front of and burned down restaurants in the past. They have thrown blood on people, and this is one of their milder tactics. I think they are a radical activist group, and I would say that they add little to responsibly addressing this issue [of animal welfare]. They simply are not a group that we feel like we can work with, and we have no intention of responding to them directly."

PETA's Violent Tactics

We're perfectly fine with PETA [People for the Ethical Treatment of Animals] exercising their First Amendment, and acting within their legal rights.

We're strong supporters of free speech and shareholders' rights, and we're glad we live in a country that protects these activities.

We are also fine with communication to us in a normal business manner, contacting us at work or through normal business channels.

But PETA has stepped over the line of protected free speech, and has resorted to pressure through intimidation, harassment, and invasion of privacy.

Let me say also this is no warm and fuzzy, garden variety animal protection group. This is not the ASPCA [American Society for the Prevention of Cruelty to Animals]. PETA's Bruce Friedrich has admitted under oath in a court of law recently that he has told his supporters at a rally that all fast food restaurants should be bombed or exploded, and he would say "Halleluja" to anyone who perpetrated these crimes.

Jonathan Blum,
testimony before the Senate Judiciary Committee,
May 18, 2004.

Although PETA's influence—or lack thereof—remains a hot topic of debate among restaurant operators, animal welfare experts seem to agree that the foodservice industry has made tremendous progress in its treatment of animals over the last five years. Reforms include updated slaughterhouse designs created to reduce animal anxiety, larger cages for egg-laying hens and much less use of cattle prods.

"I saw more changes in 1999 than I had seen previously in my whole 30-year career," says animal behaviorist Temple Grandin, who is an associate professor of animal science at Colorado State University.

McDonald's Influence

Grandin and many of her colleagues point to fast-food giant McDonald's Corp., the world's largest burger chain, as the industry's pioneer, becoming the first national chain to mandate supplier guidelines. All of its producers combined provide it with more than 2.5 billion pounds of chicken, beef and poultry annually.

In 2000 McDonald's required its egg suppliers to double the living space for each caged hen to a minimum of 72 square inches. At the time, McDonald's—which purchases some 2 billion eggs annually—also said it would no longer buy eggs from farmers who debeak chickens.

"McDonald's started setting standards with its suppliers, and then Wendy's and Burger King followed with programs of their own," says Grandin, who sits on several independent committees that oversee animal welfare for McDonald's and other large fast-food chains.

Grandin designed many of the livestock-handling facilities used in meat plants in North America and around the world, and she is considered an expert in devising ways to reduce animals' suffering and anxiety. She also developed an objective scoring system for assessing handling of cattle and pigs at meat plants that McDonald's and others have used for the basis of their audit programs.

The typical cost for upgrading facilities ranges from about $500 to $5,000 per plant, depending on its age, according to Grandin. She adds that a minority of facilities require upgrades costing $10,000 to $20,000, "but those are huge plants." She insists that most changes are simple and inexpensive, such as keeping litter off the floor, fixing broken equipment and installing better lighting.

"Animals aren't afraid of getting slaughtered, because they don't know what it is," Grandin explains. "But they are afraid of the dark and scared of shadows."

Creating a Single Program

The foodservice industry's next major step is to integrate all of the chains' various guidelines under a single system called the Animal Welfare Audit Program developed by the National Council of Chain Restaurants [NCCR], the Food Marketing Institute [FMI] and the producer community. The program, which will provide standardized data regarding animal welfare at livestock production and slaughter facilities from turkey to pork, will be fully operational by fall, according to NCCR president Terri Dort.

"Our effort was to put together a very sincere, real program that is transparent and that has accountability built into the audit," Dort explains. "Now these companies can stand up and say, 'We are committed to humane treatment of animals. End of story. Move on.'"

Many experts voice support for a consolidated audit program. Grandin explains that previously some facilities were being audited eight times a year because each restaurant chain was doing its own assessment. "Now the system will consolidate into two or three commercial audit companies," says Grandin, who adds that the best-run plants also have the highest food safety standards.

The guidelines are designed to be long-standing, and the NCCR and FMI do not plan to revise them substantially in the future in the face of anticipated and ongoing criticism from such groups as PETA. Dort emphasizes that PETA's tactics are not only "threatening" but also "counterproductive," as the industry has been working diligently to put together the auditing standards program, which has been "a major resource drain," Dort says. She adds, "The activists haven't backed off and let these companies do their work, and that's really a shame."

Questioning PETA's Goals

In fact, some observers are concerned that animal rights groups might be gaining too much clout and also are misleading the public in their goals. Wesley J. Smith, a lawyer, author and senior fellow at the Seattle-based Discovery Institute, a nonprofit public-policy think tank, says: "The agenda of animal liberationists isn't the humane, proper treatment of animals. It is the end of all use of animals. And restaurants and the food industry had better learn that."

But PETA's Friedrich says the group has no hidden agenda and is not deceiving anyone.

"Animals are not here for humans to eat," he explains. "Our ultimate goal is that other animals are not used as means to an end. That is part of our mission statement. We are a vegan group. But we are also realistic, and where we have the public on our side, we are willing to take that. Where we would like to see empty cages, in the interim we would like to see bigger cages. If we can't get animals complete freedom immediately, at least we want to make it better for them."

But Smith insists that PETA goes too far in its attempts to accelerate change.

"There is a difference between persuasion and coercion, and I think PETA crosses that line. If the industry gives into coercion, then I think it looks for more of the same because it works," Smith says.

How Restaurants Should Respond

Although PETA has faced widespread criticism of its tactics as "tasteless" and "insensitive," the group has no plans to alter the way it pressures restaurateurs.

"We are not trying to win a popularity contest as much as we are trying to improve conditions for animals," Friedrich says.

Smith advises restaurant chains to defend themselves with a two-pronged response. "No. 1 is to make sure that your ducks are in a row and that the animals are being treated appropriately under the laws, and even, if necessary, a little better than the law requires.

"And then, second, assure yourself that you cannot compromise with these fascists," he continues. "The more you give into them, the more powerful they become, and the more emboldened they are to ask for more and more and more, because the industry could never treat animals humanely enough to satisfy these people."

| "Organic farms play a vital role in sustaining and perpetuating the economic and social vibrancy of rural communities."

Organic Farming Should Be Pursued

Marika Alena McCauley and Laura Inouye

In the following viewpoint Marika Alena McCauley and Laura Inouye assert that organic farming is gaining in popularity due to Americans' increasing concern about food safety and environmental protection. According to McCauley and Inouye, organic farms are superior to traditional farms because organic farmers do not use chemicals that pollute the water, soil, and air, and the foods they produce are healthier. The authors further argue that organic farms are more profitable and provide economic benefits to farmers and their communities. McCauley is a researcher and writer and Inouye is a senior program officer at Oxfam America, the U.S. branch of Oxfam International, an organization that works to find solutions to poverty.

As you read, consider the following questions:

1. According to McCauley and Inouye, how many pounds of pesticides are used by U.S. farmers each year?

2. In the view of the authors, how does organic farming benefit farm families?

3. As described by the authors, how are pigs raised by Patchwork Family Farm?

American consumers, concerned about food safety and protecting the environment, are increasingly turning to organic foods. Growing numbers of natural food stores and mainstream grocery stores are offering organic fruits, vegetables, meat, dairy products and frozen foods, and organic farmers are making their goods directly available to consumers in their communities at farmers' markets and food stands across the country. As a result, sales of organic foods in the United States have increased by more than 20 percent every year since 1996, reaching $7.8 billion in 2000. According to the U.S. Department of Agriculture, organic cropland more than doubled during the 1990s.

Why People Are Choosing Organic Foods

Why are people going organic? Health conscious consumers and environmentalists are concerned that:

900 million pounds of pesticides are used annually by U.S. agriculture, posing threats to human health and wildlife;

24.6 million pounds of antibiotics (70 percent of total U.S. antibiotic production) are fed to chickens, pigs and cows annually. Public health authorities are finding links between such use and antibiotic-resistant bacteria which are being passed on to consumers;

Bovine growth hormones routinely given to dairy cows are linked to breast, colon and prostate cancer in humans.

Organic farming virtually excludes the use of synthetic chemicals in crop production and prohibits the use of growth hormones and antibiotics in livestock. Instead, farmers use crop rotation and organic pest management to maintain the health of their products, keeping the soil rich and productive and, most importantly, preventing toxic chemicals from poisoning consumers and from entering the water, soil and air. Organic farmers also use much less energy than their industrial counterparts. Processed organic foods contain no artificial ingredients or preservatives and are not irradiated.

Organic farms play a vital role in sustaining and perpetuating the economic and social vibrancy of rural communities. As locally based businesses, organic farms keep jobs in the community and spend farm income on local goods and services. The U.S. Department of Agriculture has conducted studies indicating that organic farms yield higher profits than conventional farms growing corn, fruits and vegetables. As these profits circulate through the local economy, they raise property values and promote investment, including tourism, in rural areas. Farm families are able to hold on to their land and can offer their children the option of continuing to work the land, decreasing the likelihood of urban migration by young people in the community.

Creating a Sustainable America

Organizations of organic farmers often take their community involvement a step further by spearheading projects to promote healthy eating, sustainable agriculture and food security. By selling directly to consumers, farmers can earn a higher price than if they went through a wholesaler, and consumers pay less than they would at a grocery store.

One Oxfam partner, Patchwork Family Farms (a project of the Missouri Rural Crisis Center), produces "pork raised the old fashioned way." Twenty family farmers raise hogs humanely, with access to fresh air and sunshine and without antibiotics or growth hormones in the feed or water. They process and market their pork collectively under their own Patchwork Family Farms label and have built up a loyal following among local food stores, restaurants, food co-ops and neighbors who stop by the office to buy fresh, healthy pork,

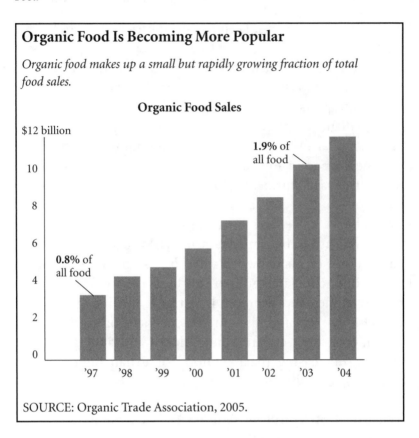

Organic Food Is Becoming More Popular

Organic food makes up a small but rapidly growing fraction of total food sales.

Organic Food Sales

SOURCE: Organic Trade Association, 2005.

ham and sausage. To order Patchwork products online, go to www.supermarketcoop.com.

By going organic, consumers not only reap health and environmental benefits, they also contribute to a more stable and sustainable rural America.

| *"Organic foods may be fresh, but they're also fresh from the manure fields."*

Organic Farming Should Not Be Pursued

John J. Miller

Foods grown on organic farms are not healthier than those grown on traditional farms, John J. Miller contends in the following viewpoint. He argues that there is no scientific evidence to support the claim that organically produced food is more nutritious. Miller also asserts that organic foods frequently contain high levels of contamination. Miller further argues that organic farming is inefficient and so could not possibly feed the world's people. Miller is the national political reporter for the National Review.

As you read, consider the following questions:

1. How many Americans become sick from food each year, according to Miller?

2. According to Norman Borlaug, as cited by Miller, what is the maximum number of people who could be fed on an all-organic diet?

3. According to the author, how many cattle would be necessary to create the amount of manure needed to support a worldwide all-organic diet?

John J. Miller, "The Organic Myth," *National Review*, February 9, 2004, pp. 35-37. Copyright © 2004 by National Review, Inc., 215 Lexington Avenue, New York, NY 10016. Reproduced by permission.

Somewhere in the cornfields of Britain, a hungry insect settled on a tall green stalk and decided to have a feast. It chewed into a single kernel of corn, filled its little belly, and buzzed off—leaving behind a tiny hole that was big enough to invite a slow decay. The agent of the decomposition was a fungus known to biologists as *Fusarium*. Farmers have a much simpler name for it: corn ear rot.

Dangerous Levels of Toxins

As the mold spread inside the corn, it left behind a cancer-causing residue called fumonisin. This sequence repeated itself thousands and thousands of times until the infested corn was harvested and sold [in 2003] as Fresh and Wild Organic Maize Meal, Infinity Foods Organic Maize Meal, and several other products.

Consuming trace amounts of fumonisin is harmless, but large doses can be deadly. [In fall 2003], the United Kingdom's Food Standards Agency detected alarming concentrations of the toxin in all six brands of organic corn meal subjected to testing—for a failure rate of 100 percent. The average level of contamination was almost 20 times higher than the safety threshold Europeans have set for fumonisin. The tainted products were immediately recalled from the food chain. In contrast, inspectors determined that 20 of the 24 non-organic corn meal products they examined were unquestionably safe to eat.

Despite this, millions of people continue to assume that organic foods are healthier than non-organic ones, presumably because they grow in pristine settings free from icky chemicals and creepy biotechnology. This has given birth to an energetic political movement. In 2002, activists in Oregon sponsored a ballot initiative that essentially would have required the state to slap biohazard labels on anything that wasn't produced in ways deemed fit by anti-biotech agitators. Voters rejected it, but the cause continues to percolate. Hawaiian legislators are giving serious thought to banning biotech crop tests in their state. In March [2004], California's Mendocino County may outlaw biotech plantings altogether. [Voters approved the ban.]

Organic Food Is Not Safer

Beneath it all lurks the belief that organic food is somehow better for us. In one poll, two-thirds of Americans said that organic food is healthier. But they're wrong: It's no more nutritious than food fueled by industrial fertilizers, sprayed with synthetic pesticides, and genetically altered in science labs. And the problem isn't limited to the fungal infections that recently cursed organic corn meal in Britain; bacteria are a major source of disease in organic food as well. To complicate matters further, organic farming is incredibly inefficient. If its appeal ever grew beyond the boutique, it would pose serious threats to the environment. Consumers who go shopping for products emblazoned with the USDA's "organic" seal of approval aren't really helping themselves or the planet—and they're arguably hurting both.

Here's the good news: At no point in human history has food been safer than it is today, despite occasional furors like the recent one over an isolated case of mad-cow disease here in the U.S. People still get sick from food—each year, about 76 million Americans pick up at least a mild illness from what they put in their mouths—but modern agricultural methods have sanitized our fare to the point where we may eat without fear. This is true for all food, organic or otherwise.

And that raises a semantic question: What is it about organic food that makes it "organic"? The food we think of as non-organic isn't really *in* organic, as if it were composed of rocks and minerals. In truth, everything we eat is organic—it's just not "organic" the way the organic-food movement has come to define the word.

Higher Levels of Contamination

A recent comparative analysis of organic produce versus conventional produce from the University of Minnesota shows that the organically grown produce had 9.7 percent positive samples for the presence of generic E. coli bacteria versus only 1.6 percent for conventional produce on farms in Minnesota.

The study, which was published in May [2004] in the *Journal of Food Protection*, concluded, "the observation that the prevalence of E. coli was significantly higher in organic produce supports the idea that organic produce is more susceptible to fecal contamination." In addition, the study found the food-borne disease pathogen salmonella only on the samples of organic produce.

Marc Morano, NewsMax,
August 2004.

About a decade ago, the federal government decided to wade into this semantic swamp. There was no compelling reason for this, but Congress nonetheless called for the invention of a National Organic Rule. It became official in 2002. Organic food, said the bureaucrats, is produced without synthetic fertilizers, conventional pesticides, growth hormones, genetic engineering, or germ-killing radiation. There are also varying levels of organic-ness: Special labels are available for products that are "made with organic ingredients" (which means the food is 70 percent organic), "organic" (which means 95 percent organic), and "100 percent organic." It's not at all clear what consumers are supposed to do with this information. As the Department of Agriculture explains on its website, the "USDA makes no claims that organically produced food is safer or more nutritious than conventionally produced food."

It doesn't because it can't: There's no scientific evidence whatsoever showing that organic food is healthier. . . .

The Costs of Organic Food

There are, in fact, good reasons to eat organic food. Often it's yummier—though this has nothing to do with the fact that it's "organic." If an organic tomato tastes better than a non-organic one, the reason is usually that it has been grown locally, where it has ripened on the vine and taken only a day or two to get from the picking to the selling. Large-scale farming operations that ship fruits and vegetables across the country or the world can't compete with this kind of homegrown quality, even though they do make it possible for people in Minnesota to avoid scurvy by eating oranges in February. Conventional produce is also a good bargain because organic foods can be expensive—the profit margins are quite high, relative to the rest of the food industry.

Unfortunately, money isn't always the sole cost. Although the overwhelming majority of organic foods are safe to eat, they aren't totally risk-free. Think of it this way: Organic foods may be fresh, but they're also fresh from the manure fields. . . .

Wasteful and Unsustainable

The very worst thing about organic farming requires the use of a word that doomsaying environmentalists have practically trademarked: It's not *sustainable*. Few activities are as wasteful as organic farming. Its yields are about half of what conventional farmers expect at harvest time. Norman Borlaug, who won the Nobel Peace Prize in 1970 for his agricultural innovations, has said, "You couldn't feed more than 4 billion people" on an all-organic diet.

If organic-food consumers think they're making a political statement when they eat, they're correct: They're declaring themselves to be not only friends of population control, but also enemies of environmental conservation. About half the world's land area that isn't covered with ice or sand is devoted to food production. Modern farming techniques have enabled this limited supply to produce increasing quantities of food. . . .

There's one more important reason that organics can't feed the world: There just isn't enough cow poop to go around. For fun, pretend that U.N. [United Nations] secretary-general Kofi Annan chowed on some ergot rye, decreed that all of humanity must eat nothing but organic food, and that all of humanity responded by saying, "What the heck, we'll give it a try." Forget about the population boom ahead. The immediate problem would be generating enough manure to fertilize all the brand-new, low-yield organic crop fields. There are a little more than a billion cattle in the world today, and each bovine needs between 3 and 30 acres to support it. Conservative estimates say it would take around 7 or 8 billion cattle to produce sufficient heaps of manure to sustain our all-organic diets. The United States alone would need about a billion head (or rear, to be precise). The country would be made up of nothing but cities and manure fields—and the experiment would give a whole new meaning to the term "fruited plains."

This is the sort of future the organic-food movement envisions—and its most fanatical advocates aren't planning to win any arguments on the merits or any consumers on the quality of organic food.

"Many small- to medium-sized commodity farmers do depend on subsidies to survive."

Farm Subsidies Should Be Preserved

Karl Beitel

In the following viewpoint Karl Beitel argues that many of the claims made against farm subsidies are inaccurate. According to Beitel, farm subsidies do not lead to declining crop prices, cause overproduction, or depress the income of farmers in developing countries. He asserts that eliminating subsidies would harm smaller farms while giving large farms greater economic power. Beitel is a policy analyst at Food First/Institute for Food and Development Policy.

As you read, consider the following questions:

1. What two facts stand out when the real prices of crops are examined, according to Beitel?
2. What is overproduction, as defined by the author?
3. As stated by the author, why would removing subsidies increase the competitive advantage of large farms?

[S ince 2000], groups spanning the ideological spectrum have come out in opposition to US and EU [European Union] farm support payments, or subsidies. Critics of US and EU farm policy claim that subsidies are a major cause of overproduction. Overproduction depresses global prices, leading to a loss of economic viability and the destruction of small-scale agriculture, both in the US and globally. While US farm policy is highly discriminatory against smaller farmers, the excessive focus on subsidies has served to obscure the deeper forces underlying the long-term decline in global farm commodity prices. This [viewpoint] will argue that declining agricultural commodity prices are rooted in the market's lack of self-correcting mechanisms. Even in the absence of subsidies, commodity markets do not tend to equilibrium or operate to ensure fair returns on farm labor. Recognizing this reality is essential to any sound reform of US commodity policy.

Two Misconceptions About Subsidies

On the surface, the argument against subsidies is quite compelling. Reforms in US farm policy instituted after 1996 established subsidy programs in which payments to farmers are triggered once prices fall below a floor price (the *loan rate*), which is set by Congress. While these subsidies shelter US farms from risk, critics argue that the floor prices encourage overproduction, generating surpluses that are then dumped on the international market at prices well below the cost of production. In fact, critics claim, the main beneficiaries of subsidy payments are not farmers, but large agribusiness firms, whose access to a steady supply of cheap farm commodities reduces their costs and boosts their profits (as they don't pass through full cost savings to consumers). This line of reasoning leads to the assumption that reducing subsidies would curb overproduction and boost prices. Critics further note, correctly, that US agricultural tariffs are higher than those levied by developing countries, and call for their reduction.

Without question, the current US subsidy system discriminates systematically against small farmers in the US and globally. But two linked misconceptions pervade the present subsidy debate: that subsidies are a principal—even *the* principal—cause of overproduction and falling prices; and, hence, that removing subsidies (and cutting tariffs) will significantly boost incomes for poor farmers in the developing world. Both these claims are inaccurate, and serve to obscure our understanding of the types of reforms that are required to restore real equity and long-term sustainability to the US and global farm economy.

Why Prices Decline

Myth # 1: Subsidies Are a Primary Cause of Declining Prices. It is true that subsidies sustain production even as prices fall below the cost of production. But claims that subsidies are a primary cause of declining prices are confusing; the reality is more complex.

In part, the present confusion over the real effect of subsidies on price results from a failure to take a longer-term view of the US farm sector. When we examine the real, inflation-adjusted prices for several major US commodity crops over the last sixty years, two facts stand out: that these prices have declined steadily over sixty years; and that the price decline since 1996 has been far less severe than in previous periods, such as the years 1973 to 1986. These two facts suggest that other factors underlie the longer-term decline, and that we must be careful in attributing recent trends in price chiefly to subsidies.

Furthermore, a 1998 upsurge in subsidy payments was triggered in response to falling prices, not the other way around. And prices fell not because of subsidies, but because the remaining vestiges of supply management programs were phased out in 1996, leading to increased competitive pressures on the supply side of the market. Clearly, we cannot explain falling prices and stressed conditions in the global farm economy simply by pointing to the market-distorting effects of US commodity subsidies.

Subsidies Do Not Lead to Overproduction

Myth # 2: Subsidies Are a Primary Cause of Overproduction. By keeping afloat farms that currently sell goods at below production costs, subsidies can indeed contribute to higher overall supply. But they are not the primary cause of overproduction; nor is excess supply the primary cause of falling prices and faltering farm incomes. Again, we need a more nuanced account of the actual causal effects.

Overproduction refers to a situation in which current supply exceeds current demand. Excess inventories accumulate, and prices fall. If overproduction caused the longer-term price decline, we would expect to see excess inventories rising as prices fall. But inventories (in relation to usage) have remained constant or fallen for all major commodity crops (corn, rice, wheat, soy, and cotton) since the early 1980s. Thus falling prices do not appear to be caused by overproduction, either before or after the 1996 subsidies were enacted. And (with the possible exception of cotton), this data offers no compelling evidence that subsidies as such are causing stocks to rise.

Critics might argue that subsidy-fueled overproduction is being exported, or "dumped" overseas, and that's why we don't have climbing surpluses at home. The data don't appear to support this theory either: both the percentage of total domestic production that is exported and the US' overall share of total world exports are either constant or falling for almost all major US commodity groups since the early 1980s—including the period after 1996.

Farm Incomes						
				Dollars per household		
					Off-Farm Earnings	
Item	Total households (number)	Mean household income	Farm Earnings	Total	Earned	Unearned
Large family farms	85,155	70,194	37,182	33,011	18,915	14,096
Very large family farms	62,199	213,982	181,660	32,321	20,407	11,914
All family farms	2,092,772	64,465	5,571	58,894	43,286	15,608

SOURCE: USDA, Economic Research Service, Agricultural Resource Management Survey, 2001.

No Help to Poor Farmers

Myth # 3: Removing US Subsidies Would Boost Farmer Incomes Worldwide. To support the claim that eliminating US subsidies would boost both world commodity prices and farmer incomes in the developing world, critics cite studies that model the effects of phasing out US and EU farm supports on global output and prices. But since these models rest on different assumptions, each yields different results—some estimating world price increases of 1.8 to 3.7 percent over ten to fifteen years, others, that prices would decrease up to 3 percent. Even the best case would lead to modest price increases and very limited benefits to select farmers.

So if subsidies are not driving declining commodity prices, what is? If eliminating subsidies won't really help poor farmers, what will?

Lower Prices Lead to Higher Output

In most major industrial sectors, the market works basically like this: a few dominant firms exercise significant control over price. Firms observe one another, getting to know their competitors' behavior. They tend to avoid price competition, using non-price means to increase their market share. The farm sector is very different. Many individual farmers supply a given market. No single farmer controls enough of the total market to influence price by adjusting his or her own supply. Instead, farmers have to take the market price as given and adjust their output accordingly.

To break even, farmers must at least be able to cover their fixed costs. Therefore, they will not, as a rule, respond to falling prices by taking land out of production—that is, working to raise prices by limiting supply. Just the opposite: confronted with falling prices, farmers will attempt to increase output in hopes of offsetting falling per-unit revenues by a higher total volume of unit sales. Failure to do so will put them out of business—sooner rather than later.

So the normal operation of the market—which aggregates the decisions of many individuals—is for lower prices to trigger higher output, leading to even lower prices. The farmer's imperative to cover fixed costs, and the fact that farmers generally do not coordinate their individual actions prior to bringing their goods to market, gives rise to the seeming irrationality of farmers' responding to falling prices by trying to increase output. And since the demand for most food goods is relatively unresponsive to price, a significant decline in price may be required to clear the market of excess supply. Thus the overall price level tends consistently downward—and buyers' expectations of what they will have to pay adjust ever downward, too.

One additional feature of the commodities market is critical to understanding both the downward trend in commodity prices and a likely effect of eliminating US farm subsidies. On average, it's true that farmers in the US regularly sell goods at prices below their costs of production. But this doesn't mean all farms in a given sector are operating at a loss. Detailed studies by the USDA [U.S. Department of Agriculture] indicate that in most major US commodity sectors, larger farms continued to post positive net returns through 2001 (the last year for which relevant data is available). These producers—the large commercial growers—set the market standard for price: as their costs fall, market prices can fall below the average US farmer's cost.

Large growers' ability to "beat the market" means that removing subsidies could actually improve their competitive advantage. Furthermore, though subsidy payments favor large growers, many small- to medium-sized commodity farmers do depend on subsidies to survive. Cutting subsidies to these farmers would accelerate farm consolidation.

Deregulation Is Not the Answer

The commodities market by itself will never guarantee farmers a price that will cover their costs, because it cannot correct itself in the ways other market sectors can. Deregulating this market further—which is what eliminating subsidies would entail—will not and cannot defend the existence of small- to medium-sized family farms, either in the US or abroad.

"Subsidies inflate the cost of farmland so that everybody loses."

Farm Subsidies Should Be Eliminated

Dennis T. Avery

In the following viewpoint Dennis T. Avery contends that the United States and Europe should stop subsidizing farmers. According to Avery, subsidies discourage farmers from using all their land in order to limit yields and get higher prices. He also argues that subsidizing organic farms, as the European Union has started to do, will destroy wildlands. Organic farming is inefficient and requires more land than does traditional farming, he claims. Avery is the director of the Hudson Institute's Center for Global Food Issues.

As you read, consider the following questions:

1. Farmers are what percentage of the U.S. working population, according to Avery?

2. According to the author, if large-scale organic farming is pursued, how long will it take for the planet's wildlands to vanish?

3. What have been the benefits of the green revolution, in Avery's opinion?

Dennis T. Avery, "Are Meat Eaters Starving the Poor?," *Ideas on Liberty*, October 2002, pp. 22-24. Copyright 2002 Foundation for Economic Education, Incorporated. www.fee.org. All rights reserved. Reproduced by permission.

Richard Tolman, head of America's National Corn Growers Association, recently told the *Wall Street Journal*, "Farm supports [subsidies] are essential to keep farmers in business so the food supply can be constant and affordable."

Farmers Are Thriving

This is an old, blatant, self-interested lie. America's farm families already make more money than their city cousins. U.S. farm families in the dust-bowl days earned only about 40 percent as much as off-farm families, but in recent years farm families have earned about 15 percent more than their city cousins—and built roughly twice as much wealth.

They could make even more if they had the courage to pursue free trade. With free trade, their exports of food and feed for the increasingly affluent consumers in land-short Asia would be hugely increased—to the benefit of North American farmers, Asian consumers, and Asia's species-rich wildlands.

Seventy years of farm subsidies have not kept the number of U.S. farmers from shrinking radically, even as technology increased yields and sharply lowered their real costs of production. Today, U.S. farmers number less than 2 percent of the working population. The farming story is the same in Europe and around the world (excepting mainly Africa).

A Political Ploy

Farm subsidies are just a way for politicians to buy votes. City people accept farm subsidies because of the constant public whining of people like Tolman. Subsidies inflate the cost of farmland so that everybody loses—especially Third World consumers, First World taxpayers, and young farmers everywhere.

Nevertheless, the twenty-first century looks as though it's becoming a new heyday for farm subsidies. America's brand-new farm bill may cost another $80 billion in payments to its farmers over seven years. The new farm law ends a short-lived experiment with market-set prices for farmers (dating only from 1996) and slips the country's big commercial farmers back into that cash-filled congressional pocket. (The production-based subsidies don't do much for the small farmers, since they don't produce much.)

Across the Atlantic, the European Union [EU] has announced yet another "reform" in the name of Europe's centuries-old tradition of protecting its "peasant" farmers from foreign competition. The EU says it will now stop paying for farm surpluses and instead shift its subsidies toward making its farmers more environmentally sustainable (meaning organic). Since organic farming is actually less sustainable (and much lower yielding) than conventional farming, the new EU policy is another political lie. It is being advanced to prevent the governmentally unthinkable: ending the farm spending that takes up half of the EU budget and (gasp) giving all that money back to Europe's taxpayers.

A Loss of First World Jobs

The EU says it will instead extend its new, greener, but equally expensive Common Agricultural Policy (CAP) to another 10 new member nations over the next few years. At least 4 of these countries (Poland, Hungary, Romania, and Bulgaria) are potentially important farm producers. But extending the CAP to millions of additional farmers could double the EU's farm subsidy costs again within a decade. Will Germany, the farm programs' cash cow, stand for that?

Meanwhile, the World Trade Organization has failed to liberalize the world's pervasive farm trade barriers. While the average tariff on nonfarm products has been cut from about 40 to 4 percent since the world's big trade liberalization effort was launched in 1948, the average tariff on farm products is still somewhere above 60 percent.

Behind the appearance of pork-barrel politics as usual, today's First World farmers are paying a high price for their

Subsidies Are Bad for the Environment

Thanks to U.S. price supports, agricultural economist Del Gardner notes, "land has been cultivated ... that would have remained in rangeland and forests, especially in the southern region and in the semi-arid and arid regions of the Great Plains and Rocky Mountains." "Aided by government farm programs," writes John Hosemann, retired chief economist of the American Farm Bureau, "farmers clearcut and drained large tracts of forestland, particularly in the Mississippi River delta region but also in the mid-Atlantic states." In the Florida Everglades, over half a million acres of swamplands have been converted to sugar fields to take advantage of government subsidies.

Subsidies also lead to increased use of chemical inputs. In a study of six farming states, Jonathan Tolman found that eliminating subsidies would reduce fertilizer use by 29 percent.

J. Bishop Grewell, American Enterprise,
October/November 2003.

"free" government money. They are giving up huge export market potential, at a moment when more and more of the densely populated Third World is gaining income and demanding better diets. China doubled its meat consumption in eight years during the 1990s. Ice cream is the latest food fad in Beijing, China, and New Delhi, India; neither country has the pastures to support more dairy cattle. By retreating back into subsidies instead of selling high-value exports, the First World's subsidized farmers are costing their rural communities both farming and farming-support jobs. By accepting government payments for millions of acres of "set-aside land," U.S. and European farmers are literally running their own kids and neighbors out of town. What should today be thriving rural communities, supplying high-value farm commodities and processed foods to eager export buyers, instead feature boarded-up stores and shriveling school enrollments.

Problems Ahead for Subsidies

The new U.S. farm subsidy outlays were a frantic congressional response to a 50-50 split between the two parties in the 2000 elections, razor-thin margins of control in the House and Senate, and the illusion of a federal budget surplus. (The bill was written and commitments obtained before [the September 11, 2001, terrorist attacks].) Now, however, the U.S. government is facing a 2002 deficit of $150 billion—and the reality that Social Security reform could force Congress to renege on its farm-spending promises.

Europe's announcement that it will abandon the commercial farmers it created and encouraged through its farm production subsidies since 1965 should come as no surprise. Its commercial farmers, quite rationally, continue to produce surpluses in response to high government-supported prices. Europe's city folks are tired of (1) paying to grow the chemically intensive surpluses and (2) paying again to subsidize them into export markets.

Worse, a major group of Third World countries told the World Trade Organization's meeting [in 2002] that Europe would have to agree to a phaseout of its farm export subsidies or it would accept no new negotiations on lowering nonfarm trade barriers. As nonfarm trade is now much more important to the EU than farming trade, the EU gave in.

Meanwhile, activists and opportunistic politicians, playing off the very real fear of mad cow disease, have whipped European consumers into frenzied fear of their own food supply. Mad cow has claimed only about two dozen victims, but the media have cheerfully published estimates that ranged into hundreds of thousands. The European reaction has been to reject the science-based technology that failed to foresee that a piece of DNA biologists didn't know existed (a prion) would jump across two species (sheep and cattle) to attack a few humans with a brain disease the world had never before encountered.

Europe's elites now believe they can relieve their food safety worries, keep lots of small farms, and get rid of their high costs of farm export subsidies with one policy masterstroke: going organic. They hope that "green" payments to small farmers and heavy taxes on fertilizers and pesticides will reduce Europe's farm output to match what Europe eats. (They're ignoring the health risks of fertilizing all their food crops with pathogen-laden cattle manure.) . . .

Protecting Wildlands

The world is already farming nearly half the planet's land not covered by glaciers or deserts. If we shift back to organic farming, virtually all of the planet's wildlands will be cleared for low-yield crops and cattle forage within 20 years.

Fortunately, we have proven alternatives: higher, more-sustainable yields based on science and technology, and more farm exports from good croplands to densely populated countries.

Science has already given us the green revolution, which tripled the yields on most of the world's good cropland, saved a billion people from famine, and prevented 12 million square miles of wildlands from being plowed for low-yield crops. Fortunately too, we still have the science institutions that produced the green revolution, though we've been starving them of funds because high yields have been politically incorrect. (America's public funding for agricultural research has declined by one-third since 1960, and the biggest set of Third World agricultural research centers gets a puny $340 million per year.) High-yield conservation also works in forestry. Managed forests can produce 20 times as much wood per year as a wild forest, enormously reducing logging pressure on the wild forests' biodiversity. Moreover, wood is our most ecofriendly and renewable building material.

High-Yield Heroes

All this explains why two Nobel Peace Prize winners, a cofounder of Greenpeace, a major U.S. presidential candidate, and the latest World Food Prize winner recently became founding signers of the "Declaration in Support of Protecting Nature with High-Yield Farming and Forestry."

The founding signers:

- Norman Borlaug, green revolution plant breeder and 1970 Nobel Peace Prize winner.

- Oscar Arias, former president of Costa Rica, 1986 Nobel Peace laureate, and currently ambassador for the Third World network of agricultural research stations.

- Patrick Moore, forestry expert and cofounder of Greenpeace.

- Former Senator George McGovern, recently the United Nations' "ambassador to the hungry."

- James Lovelock, British chemist and author of *The Gaia Hypothesis.*

- Per Pinstrup-Anderson, development economist and 2001 World Food Prize winner.

- Eugene Lapointe, president of the World Conservation Trust.

- Former Sen. Rudy Boschwitz, advisory chairman of the Hudson Institute Center for Global Food Issues.

These "high-yield heroes" signed their names and huge reputations to a politically incorrect strategy because it is the only visible way to avoid massive famines, billions of forced abortions for a whole generation of the world's young women, and/or the wholesale destruction of forests, wild species, and ecosystems.

The Real Choice Farmers Face

Unfortunately, the *Washington Post*, *USA Today*, and the *New York Times*, which cheerfully give their front pages to activists dressed like butterflies and the self-interested pleadings of well-off farmers, couldn't find space for the High-Yield Conservation story. If you asked their editors, they might even tell you they didn't want to undercut the "environmental movement."

Farming's real choice is not whether to feed people. The people will be fed. The real choice is whether to save the wildlands. Farm subsidies stand in the way of doing both.

Periodical Bibliography

Geoffrey Cowley	"Certified Organic," *Newsweek*, September 30, 2002.
Rod Dreher	"USDA-Disapproved: Small Farmers and Big Government," *National Review*, January 27, 2003.
J. Bishop Grewell	"Farm Subsidies Are Harm Subsidies," *American Enterprise*, October/November 2003.
Brian Halweil	"Eating at Home," *Ode*, May 2005.
David Hosansky	"Farm Subsidies," *CQ Researcher*, May 17, 2002.
Hilary Mertaugh	"Concentration in the Agri-Food System," *Left Turn*, August/September 2003.
Marc Morano	"Organic Food Has 'Significantly Higher' Contamination," *NewsMax*, August 2004.
Danielle Nierenberg	"The Commercialization of Farming," *USA Today Magazine*, January 2004.
Jay Nordlinger	"PETA vs. KFC," *National Review*, December 22, 2003.
Joel Novek	"Something Smells," *Alternatives Journal*, Fall 2003.
Robert J. Samuelson	"A Sad Primer in Hypocrisy," *Newsweek*, February 11, 2002.

OPPOSING
VIEWPOINTS®
SERIES

CHAPTER 3

What Causes Obesity?

Chapter Preface

Being overweight in the United States is now the norm: 55 percent of adult Americans are either overweight or obese. With millions of Americans carrying excess weight, there is little surprise that the causes of obesity have been hotly debated. Possible factors contributing to obesity include advertising that makes high-fat and high-sugar foods especially appealing, schools that stock their vending machines with candy and soda, and parental influence. In some cases, however, obesity may be unavoidable—various studies have suggested that dozens of genes could be linked to weight gain. Two genes that have received particular attention are the melanocortin 4 receptor gene and the GAD2 gene.

Studies have found that mutations in both genes can lead to overeating, and many researchers claim that obese people are more likely to have faulty versions of the genes. A March 2003 article in the *New England Journal of Medicine* detailed the findings of a Swiss-German-American study on the melanocortin 4 receptor gene and its effect on the hypothalamus, the part of the brain that regulates hunger. The gene creates a protein that helps stimulate appetite in the hypothalamus. If a person possesses a mutated version of the gene, he or she will feel abnormally hungry. Consequently, people with the faulty gene gain weight because they overeat in response to the constant hunger pangs. The journal also included the findings of a British team of researchers who discovered that a mutation of the melanocortin 4 receptor gene was present in more than 5 percent of the five hundred severely obese children they studied.

The GAD2 gene can also lead to overeating if it is mutated, many researchers say. The gene helps produce GABA, a neurotransmitter that is involved with appetite stimulation. According to a study of more than twelve hundred people conducted by an international group of researchers, increased levels of GABA (caused by a mutated GAD2 gene) may lead to hunger and overeating. The researchers assert that the faulty gene may be the cause of obesity for up to 10 percent of seriously overweight people. As the author of the research, professor Philippe Froguel, from Institut Pasteur in Lille, France, explains, "The discovery that this one gene plays a role in determining whether someone is likely to overeat could be crucial in understanding the continued rise in obesity rates around the world."

These studies have been criticized by other researchers, however, who have concluded that the two genes have little, if any, correlation to obesity. For example, a team of European and American scientists studied Swedish and American subjects, both obese and non-obese, and did not find a link between the melanocortin 4 receptor gene and obesity. An August 2005 article by the journal *Public Library of Science Biology* detailed the findings from another study on GAD2. The researchers could not find a significant statistical link between obesity and a mutated GAD2 gene.

The role that genes play in determining why people become obese is only one of the debates surrounding the increasingly serious problem of obesity. In the following chapter the authors evaluate other causes of obesity. Biological, cultural, and social factors may all play significant roles in weight problems.

> *"Designating obesity as a distinct disease . . . would permit millions of Americans to get the help they now lack."*

Obesity Is a Disease

Steven Findlay

Americans would benefit if the U.S. government were to label obesity a disease, Steven Findlay asserts in the following viewpoint. He contends that designating obesity a disease would spur research into treating and preventing weight gain and enable millions of Americans to receive insurance coverage and medical help for obesity-related problems. Findlay further argues that obesity is the result of both genetics and poor behavioral choices, and concludes that solving the problem will require not only assistance from the government and medical community but from businesses and communities as well. Findlay is a health policy analyst.

As you read, consider the following questions:

1. According to Findlay, what percentage of American adults are overweight or obese?
2. What is the likelihood of a child becoming obese if both parents are thin, according to the author?
3. In the author's view what will be the biggest challenge if obesity is designated as a disease?

You have no doubt heard: Obesity is fast becoming public health enemy No. 1. We are big and getting bigger. We have super-sized, fat-snacked and couch-slouched our way to a serious health crisis. This threatens to reverse the hard-won gains we've made during the past 30 years: lower rates of heart-disease deaths, longer life expectancy and healthier aging.

In 1980, about 45% of U.S. adults were overweight or obese. That rose to 55% in 1990. Today, the proportion is 65% (half of whom are obese, meaning about 30 pounds or more above a healthy weight for their height). Yes, an incredible two-thirds of U.S. adults weigh too much. So do many of our children. Fifteen percent of 6- to 19-year-olds—about 9 million—are overweight, up from 10% a decade ago. The price tag is about $120 billion a year in medical expenses and lost productivity.

Scientific and Medical Support

Opinion varies widely about what to do. The newest recommendation came earlier [in December 2003] when a government-convened panel of experts recommended that doctors weigh and measure all their adult patients and refer obese ones to intensive counseling and behavioral treatment.

That's welcome advice, but it falls short of the decisive action needed to kick-start a more serious response to this epidemic: designating obesity as a distinct disease. The IRS did so in 2002, so taxpayers could deduct the cost of weight-loss programs prescribed by a doctor. And federal health officials and private-sector health groups have been reviewing the issue for months. As with alcoholism and drug addiction, this step would permit millions of Americans to get the help they now lack because of limits in public and private insurance coverage. It would put obesity prevention and treatment research and drug development on new footings. And it gradually would alter public perceptions of the condition.

Although not without controversy, mounting scientific evidence and medical consensus supports the move. Genetics is the foundation. Studies of twins indicate that about 50% to 70% of the tendency toward obesity is inherited. Likewise, studies show that when both parents are obese, the chance their offspring also will be obese is 60% to 80%. In contrast, when both parents are thin, the likelihood of a child becoming obese is 9%.

Lifestyle Plays a Role

The emerging theory is that the genetic tendency to obesity is both metabolic and behavioral. In other words, obesity occurs mostly because of disturbances in the body's regulation of fat and calories, but also because of biologically based abnormalities in food cravings, satiety and eating patterns.

Skeptical opponents assert four things: (a) that plain old overeating and inactivity are the chief causes of obesity (even in people with a genetic "propensity"); (b) that the gene pool hasn't changed in the past 20 years, but eating habits have; (c) that not all obese people are unhealthy; and (d) that "medicalizing" obesity will detract from public health efforts focused on individual responsibility for one's weight.

But most diseases today, including heart disease, cancer, stroke and AIDS, are partly if not significantly due to lifestyle and behavioral choices. Obesity is the end result of poor lifestyle and genetics in the same way that lung cancer or heart attacks can be the end result of smoking and genetics. And there's growing evidence that all obese people are at higher risk of premature death, similar to all people who have elevated cholesterol levels, which is declared a medical condition worthy of professional care.

All of that said, if and when obesity is deemed a disease, the biggest challenge will be drawing the line between obesity and plain everyday overweight. There's no evidence that the latter is primarily driven by genetics, especially for people who

A Steady Increase in Obesity

The number of people who are overweight, obese, and morbidly obese has increased steadily during the past 20 years. The Centers for Disease Control and Prevention began collecting measured heights and weights of adults in 1960. According to these data, the prevalence of people who are overweight and obese in the United States was relatively stable between 1960 and 1980; however, rates have been on the rise since then.

In 1978, the National Institutes of Health classified morbid obesity as a disease. It also defined the "hazards it poses to life, health, and well being." Results of the 1999 to 2000 National Health and Nutrition Examination Survey indicate that an estimated 65% of US adults are either overweight or obese. This is an increase from 47% of adults ages 20 to 74 years estimated to be overweight in the 1976 to 1980 survey and 56% of adults in the same age group estimated to be overweight in the 1988 to 1994 survey.

Janet Shortt, AORN Journal, *December 2004.*

are carrying around an extra 5–7 pounds or so. Today's cutoffs based on the body mass index (BMI) scale are simple and useful, but doctors and insurers will have to make judgments. Clearer guidelines must be set.

A Large-Scale Response

Separating the obese from the purely overweight and medically targeting the former does not get us off the hook from more aggressively attacking all of America's excess poundage. There's a raging debate now about who is to blame, and the lawsuit mill has begun. This is mostly a waste of energy and time. We are all to blame: It's a broad social failure, a cultural milieu that backfired, big time.

The larger solution lies in every institution and individual doing his or her part. Some are moving in the right direction. Food companies such as Kraft are pledging to make healthier snacks. Fast-food chains are promising new low-fat choices and say they will alter their ingredients. Large employers are taking a new look at work-site counseling. Health plans and doctors are initiating new prevention, treatment and weight-management programs. Communities are talking about more walking and bike trails and kids' after-school-activity programs. The Food and Drug Administration is poised to make food labels clearer. State legislators introduced some 150 measures in 2003 addressing the problem, twice [2002's] number. Individuals are taking responsibility.

But even larger-scale social action is needed. As with the public-health response to infectious diseases, smoking, auto safety and traffic deaths due to drunken driving, once the evidence becomes clear, we must kick into high gear. That means firm government regulation and changes in behavior, both voluntary and altered by law (think smoking in public places).

The problem is that this process can take years. Declaring obesity a disease would be a strong first step toward accelerating our response to the epidemic of excess fat in our diets, on our bodies and in our body politic.

We are earth's richest nation and in many ways its most creative. Let's not be its fattest.

"By making obesity a disease, govern-
ment does all Americans—large or
not—a disservice."

Obesity Is Not a Disease

Sonia Arrison

Obesity should not be labeled a disease, Sonia Arrison contends
in the following viewpoint. She asserts that while obesity is be-
coming more prevalent in the United States, treating it as an ill-
ness instead of the result of poor dietary choices would unfairly
harm healthy Americans. By calling obesity a disease, the condi-
tion could be treated using Medicare or Medicaid funds, which
come from the taxpayer dollars of all Americans, fat or thin. Ar-
rison concludes that individuals must be aware of the conse-
quence of their overeating and realize that society will not pay
for their higher health care costs. Arrison is the director of tech-
nology studies at the Pacific Research Institute, a public policy
think tank that promotes free-market solutions.

As you read, consider the following questions:

1. What percentage of U.S. medical expenditures in 1998
   was due to obesity, as stated by the author?

2. In Arrison's opinion what is the result when individuals
   are encouraged to ignore the effects of an unhealthy
   lifestyle?

3. What lesson about health does the author think children need to learn?

[In March 2005] California Governor Arnold Schwarzenegger announced his intentions to support a bill outlawing the sale of junk food in schools. Science shows the governor is right to worry about an obesity crisis, but banning candy in schools is like putting a Band-Aid on a third-degree burn.

According to the American Obesity Association, "approximately 127 million adults in the U.S. are overweight, 60 million obese, and 9 million severely obese." That's a huge number of people, and basic medicine predicts that their weight problems will turn into more serious conditions such as type 2 diabetes, hypertension, heart disease, stroke, a number of cancers, gall bladder-disease, osteoarthritis and obstructive sleep apnea.

The Economics of Obesity

In short, people are eating themselves to death. While consequences are dire for each obese individual, what many don't realize is that their choices also harm the part of America that remains healthy. The most obvious impact is the economic strain. Numbers provided by the Centers for Disease Control and Prevention (CDC) show that obesity costs Americans a ton.

For instance, in 1998, medical expenses due to obesity accounted for 9.1 percent of total U.S. medical expenditures and may have been as high as $78.5 billion. That's a lot of cash, but the kicker is that approximately half of these costs were paid by Medicaid and Medicare—in other words, by taxpayers. There's something disturbing about this situation, which could be described as socialized obesity. By sharing the health care costs with obese people, health-conscious Americans lose tax dollars and see health insurance premiums shoot up.

[In 2004] Health and Human Services Secretary Tommy Thompson designated obesity as a disease. But much of obe-

The Exaggerated Health Risks of Obesity

Despite the assertions that obesity is causing our society great harm ..., many scientists and activist groups have disputed the level of danger that it actually poses. Indeed, a recent analysis presented in the *Journal of the American Medical Association* (JAMA) by Katherine Flegal of the CDC [Centers for Disease Control and Prevention] and her colleagues calls the severity of the dangers of excess body fat into question, indicating that the number of overweight and obesity-related deaths is actually about 26,000—about one fifteenth the earlier estimate of 400,000.

Patrick Johnson, Skeptical Inquirer, *September/October 2005.*

sity is caused by poor nutrition and behavioral problems. By making obesity a disease, government does all Americans—large or not—a disservice. Many diseases hit individuals through no fault of their own, but obesity is in a different category.

Individual Responsibility

To ward off obesity, proper diet and exercise are necessary. Yet the socialization of the costs of the problem only makes it more likely that individuals will carry on with their destructive behavior. It's not rocket science: Whatever is subsidized will grow. And by incentivizing individuals to ignore the consequences of an unhealthy lifestyle, we all suffer a productivity hit when otherwise smart people die early due to obesity-related diseases. Dr. Bruce Ames, the eminent biochemist and inventor of the Ames test for carcinogens, has made longevity and diet one of his key areas of study. His conclusions show that in order to live longer, individuals must maintain a good diet, including the proper amount of vitamins and antioxidants. This advice might seem a no-brainer, but it is easy to ignore in a society where junk food marketing is everywhere and the costs of individual overeating are distributed amongst everyone.

The best way to help mitigate the onslaught of obesity is to make sure that individuals are aware that the costs of their behavior will be borne by them. That is, if they choose to eat potato chips and sit in front of the television night after night, instead of eating fruits and vegetables and exercising, then they should not expect society to help them pay the higher costs of health insurance.

Perhaps this is a cultural issue as much as a political one, which brings the discussion back to Governor Schwarzenegger's quest to ban junk food in schools. The idea of educating the population about the risks associated with empty calories, such as those found in soda, is a good one. And in a publicly-run system where government is supposed to be responsible for the well being of children, perhaps it makes sense. But there is a larger issue.

While schools should educate children about nutrition and a healthy diet, ultimately, kids will have to make their own decisions. So the lesson is also one of individual responsibility. That's how a free and healthy society operates.

| *"It is no wonder that super-size portions are leading to super-size people."*

Eating Fast Food Causes Obesity

Sharron Dalton

In the following viewpoint Sharron Dalton argues that fast-food consumption is one of the causes of obesity, particularly among school-age children. She contends that the offerings at fast-food restaurants are excessively high in fat and calories. Moreover, she maintains, "super-sizing" tricks consumers into eating larger amounts of these unhealthy foods. Dalton is an associate professor of nutrition, food studies, and public health at New York University and the author of Our Overweight Children: What Parents, Schools, and Communities Can Do to Control the Fatness Epidemic, *the source of this viewpoint.*

As you read, consider the following questions:

1. According to Eric Schlosser, what draws children to fast-food restaurants?

2. Why does the author criticize the introduction of white meat Chicken McNuggets?

3. According to Dalton, what is the calorie difference between the average cheeseburger in 1977 and 1996?

When several overweight teenagers from New York sued McDonald's, blaming the fast-food giant for their obesity and weight-related medical conditions, their case provided ample fodder in the debate over personal responsibility versus society's responsibility for causing and curbing fatness. The plaintiffs in the suit included a teenage girl—age nineteen, 5 feet 6 inches tall, 270 pounds—who said she ate a McMuffin for breakfast and a Big Mac meal with apple pie for dinner almost daily. Another plaintiff, a fifteen-year-old boy, said he grew to 400 pounds and developed diabetes because he had eaten McDonald's food every day since he was six. A U.S. district court judge dismissed the case in early 2003 but, in recognition of their compelling arguments, left the door open for the plaintiffs to amend and refile their complaints.

The question on many people's minds was, what kind of parents would let their kids eat McDonald's food *every day*? Other questions that merit an equal level of concern and contempt come to mind: what forces are at work in the marketplace—not to mention schools and the media—to push aside healthier fare? Why are McDonald's and other fast-food outlets so available and attractive to so many Americans?

Societal and Personal Factors

The judge—who famously described Chicken McNuggets as "a McFrankenstein creation of various elements not utilized by the home cook" —noted that kids are drawn to the restaurant chain not only for its food but also for its toy promotions and playground-like play areas. His remark raises two more questions. How do the food and restaurant industries target youth through clever marketing? And what opportunities for outdoor play and recreation are missing from these kids' lives that make them flock to a McDonald's PlayPlace?

As the questions above suggest, it is the interplay of societal and personal factors—not the parents' or children's behavior alone—that is responsible for young people such as these plaintiffs growing so fat.

After reviewing the McDonald's case with my teenage students, I polled them for an opinion. Of sixty students, fifty-seven agreed with the case dismissal, calling it "absurd" or "ridiculous," because "everyone knows that fast food is unhealthy." Most students held the parents responsible; the rest blamed the plaintiffs themselves for eating foods that made them fat. If pressed to choose, I would side with the judge's dismissal, and I am concerned that lawsuits may not achieve the desired results, but I would not characterize the case as "absurd." It is unreasonable to expect parents, already overburdened, to make a lone stand against fast foods touted to their kids (even as toddlers). . . .

High-Fat and High-Calorie Meals

Americans forked over $110 billion to fast-food restaurants in 2002. These restaurants report that half of their sales are now at the drive-by window—a high volume of backseat or dashboard dining that reflects the reality of today's hurried lifestyles and poses a threat to healthy eating.

Consider, for example, the difference between breakfast at home and breakfast from a drive-through. Breakfast, we're often told, is the most important meal of the day, which is especially true for school-age children. It is potentially their healthiest, most balanced meal and provides the energy they need to be mentally alert at school—and eating breakfast helps control weight by keeping hunger in line. A breakfast of vitamin-fortified, lightly sweetened whole-grain cereal (such as Cheerios), fruit, and milk amounts to about 250–300 calories. But a child whose family swings by a McDonald's on the way to school might eat a 5.5 oz bacon, egg, and cheese biscuit (470 calories) or a 9 oz Spanish omelet bagel (680 calories). Add a couple of hash brown patties (300 calories) plus a 16 oz container of orange juice (220 calories), and the calorie total comes to around 1,000 calories. This is enough to feed four small children, two medium-size preteens, or one captain of a high school football team. The McDonald's meal, in addition to being excessively high-calorie, is a nutritional nightmare, containing high amounts of saturated fat and low amounts of the fiber, calcium, and vitamins that young (and older) bodies need. The "breakfast of champions" advertised on a Wheaties box—healthy cereal with milk and juice—is becoming a memory as high-calorie fast-food breakfasts become the norm.

In *Fast Food Nation*, Eric Schlosser uncovered the fast-food industry's efforts to reel in the youngest, most susceptible consumers. "Fast food," he claims, "has fueled an epidemic of obesity." And how does the industry reel in the kids? Why do children and their parents eat so frequently at fast-food restaurants? "That's a 'no-brainer,'" I'm told when I ask families and kids what draws them to fast-food restaurants. "They're cheap, they're nearby, we love the food because you always know exactly what you're getting—and besides, everyone else goes and gets the toys."

Schlosser describes how McDonald's and Burger King operate over 10,000 playgrounds. He interviewed "Playlands" makers, who explained "Playlands bring in children, who bring in parents, who bring in money." The seesaws and slides are effective lures but, Schlosser reports, "the key to attracting kids is toys, toys, toys." A successful promotion easily doubles or triples the weekly volume of children's meals. Ronald McDonald is a "trusted friend" of most families, recognized by 96 percent of American children.

Targeting Low-Income Neighborhoods

When I talked with people from the Bronx neighborhood who eat at the two McDonald's restaurants (only short blocks apart) sued by the teens for making them fat, it was easy to see how low-income minority neighborhoods are great "targets" for the promotions of fast-food chains. The food is

Calories and Fat Grams in Fast Food Burgers

Burger (Chain)	Calories	Fat grams
Big Mac (McDonald's)	554 calories	30 grams
Whopper (Burger King)	700 calories	42 grams
Classic Single (Wendy's)	430 calories	20 grams
Jumbo Jack (Jack in the Box)	597 calories	34.5 grams
Thickburger (Hardee's)	850 calories	57 grams

SOURCE: Calorie King, "Calorie Charts and Nutritional Information," www.calorieking.com.

cheap: "We use the coupons—buy one, get one free, like, 'Free Big Mac with purchase of a regular price Big Mac.'" "Extra Value meals give you a 32 oz soft drink [instead of 21 oz] and large fries too [instead of medium] for only 40 cents more." The place is familiar and comfortable: "My friends work here." "Cool place to hang out." The location is strategic: "McDonald's is right around the corner, open from 6 A.M. to midnight." And, above all, the food tastes good: "I love French fries—my favorite snack since I was a little kid." Yes indeed, McDonald's marketing formula reels in the young customers with taste, cost, and accessibility.

Two teens with both "size and style" told me, "Those girls who sued probably have families who work too much and don't have time to cook a well-balanced meal," and, "They do have a point about the McNuggets because the list of ingredients is so long and with things that only a nutritionist would know what it does to your body." One also noted that McDonald's has taken a few small steps toward a healthier menu: "McDonald's must be scared now because I just saw a commercial that said they have changed the McNuggets to all-white meat."

Consumers are demanding fresher ingredients and healthier choices in fast-food restaurants. As a nutritionist, I hope the move toward healthy fast food is real (all white meat and less grease), spurred by books like *Fast Food Nation* and eye-opening lawsuits. I was first delighted to see the "new all white meat chicken McNuggets" coupons appear shortly after the lawsuit hit the news—until I noticed the small print: "Only available in Manhattan south of 96th Street." Two plaintiffs in one suit live at least a forty-five-minute, two-dollar subway or bus ride away from the nearest McDonald's selling the new McNuggets, McVeggie Burgers, and the New Premium Salads with grilled chicken. Even if these healthier choices taste good and are priced right, they still are not accessible in the very neighborhood that ignited the movement toward healthier fast food. Nearly a year later, the customer representative said, "They are being test-marketed in selected stores."

The Spread of Super-Sizing

We also have the food industry to thank for the insidious super-sizing trend that has made this generation accustomed to portions that are larger and higher in calories than ever before. Consider that eating just one hundred calories more per day than needed adds about ten extra pounds in a year, and it is no wonder that super-size portions are leading to super-size people. In 1977, for example, the average cheeseburger weighed 5.8 oz and contained 397 calories; by 1996 it weighed 7.3 oz and provided 533 calories.

"Meal deals" harness the desire of customers young and old to get the most for their money. For an extra 69 cents or so, they get extralarge portions of fries and sodas, which cost the restaurant only a few pennies more to produce. "It's a great sales technique," notes [Marion] Nestle in the *Nutrition Action Healthletter*. "People buy larger sizes because they perceive them as good value. If they're going to spend all this money on food, especially in a restaurant, they figure they might as well get a lot to eat."

Super-sizing spread from restaurants and convenience stores like 7-Eleven to the grocer's shelves; between the late 1970s and 1990s, the number of large-portion-size food products increased tenfold. Old-fashioned "large" 16 oz bags of potato chips are now positively dwarfed by new "normal-size" 32 oz bags—get two for just a little more than the price of one, all in one bag! Coca Cola was sold in 6.5 oz bottles in the 1950s; single-serving 20 oz bottles are common in the new millennium. Family-size containers (64 oz) of cola are sometimes used as single servings, consumed in a few minutes by thirsty teens—and many preteens.

Super-sizing not only plays into the innate belief that bigger is better, it also manipulates the desire for food that people know is "bad" for them. Packaging unhealthy food in huge portions makes the consumer feel less guilty about eating large amounts. . . .

No Encouragement to Be Healthy

We now know why children are getting fatter. They eat excess high-sucrose/corn syrup foods (everyone is born with the liking for sweet). They learn early on to like what is offered (high-calorie foods and few low-calorie vegetables and fruits). They quickly respond to seductive cues in their environment (advertising, availability, and accessibility of food and drink an arm's reach away). They sit more than they move.

Though as a species we have evolved excellent physiological mechanisms to defend against body weight loss, we have only weak defenses against weight gain when food is abundant. Control of portion size, consumption of a diet high in fruits and vegetables and low in fat, and regular physical activity are behaviors that protect against obesity. Nothing in the current environment, however, encourages children to adopt and maintain these behaviors.

| "A fast food burger may not enhance your health . . . but it is very easy to find out how fatty that burger is."

Fast Food Should Not Be Blamed for Obesity

Todd G. Buchholz

In the following viewpoint Todd G. Buchholz argues that fast-food restaurants have been unfairly blamed for rising obesity rates. He maintains that people are gaining weight because they are snacking more at home or eating at sit-down restaurants. Moreover, according to Buchholz, consumers today have a wider choice of healthy fast-food options and therefore cannot accuse fast-food restaurants if they get fat from eating higher-fat products. Buchholz was an economic adviser in the George H.W. Bush administration.

As you read, consider the following questions:

1. Why does the author believe the rise in Body Mass Index between the nineteenth century and 1960 was a modern victory?
2. What proportion of calories is consumed at home, according to Buchholz?
3. According to the author, why have fast-food restaurants expanded their menus?

Todd G. Buchholz, "Burgers, Fries, and Lawyers," *Policy Review*, February/March 2004, pp. 45-52, 57-59. Reproduced by permission.

[In 2003] the U.S. District Court for the Southern District of New York responded to a complaint filed against McDonald's by a class of obese customers, alleging among other things that the company acted negligently in selling foods that were high in cholesterol, fat, salt, and sugar. In the past 10 years we have seen an outburst of class action lawsuits that alleged harm to buyers. With classes numbering in the thousands, these suits may bring great riches to tort lawyers, even if they provide little relief to the plaintiffs. The sheer size of the claims and the number of claimants often intimidate defending firms, which fear that their reputations will be tarnished in the media and their stock prices will be punished—not because of the merits but from the ensuing publicity. In his opinion in the McDonald's case, Judge Robert W. Sweet suggested that the McDonald's suit could "spawn thousands of similar 'McLawsuits' against restaurants." Recent books with titles like *Fat Land* and *Fast Food Nation* promote the view that fast food firms are harming our health and turning us into a people who are forced to shop in the "big and tall" section of the clothing stores. The *Wall Street Journal* recently reported that "big and tall" has become a $6 billion business in menswear, "representing more than a 10 percent share of the total men's market."

But before the legal attack on fast food gets too far along, it would be useful to look at the facts behind fast food and fat America and to ask whether the courtroom is really the place to determine what and where people should eat. . . .

The Rise in Body Mass Index

If you believe the old saying "you are what you eat," human beings are not what they used to be. Before jumping into today's fashionable condemnation of calories, let us spend a moment on historical perspective and at least admit that for mankind's first couple hundred thousand years of existence, the basic human problem was how to get enough calories and micronutrients. Forget the caveman era: As recently as 100 years ago, most people were not receiving adequate nutrition. Malnutrition was rampant, stunting growth, hindering central nervous systems, and making people more susceptible to disease. Often, poor people begged on the streets because they did not have the sheer physical energy to work at a job, even if work was available to them. By modern standards even affluent people a century ago were too small, too thin, and too feeble, as economist Robert W. Fogel has noted. A century ago, an American with some spare time and spare change was more likely to sign up for a weight-gaining class than a weight-loss program.

Just as life expectancy in the United States rose almost steadily from about 47 years in 1900 to 80 years today, so too has the "Body Mass Index," or BMI, a ratio of height to weight. In the late nineteenth century, most people died too soon and were, simply put, too skinny. The two are related, of course. For most of human history only the wealthy were plump; paintings of patrons by Peter Paul Rubens illustrated that relationship. In ancient times figurines of Venus (carved thousands of years ago) displayed chunky thighs, big bellies, and BMIs far above today's obesity levels. Likewise, skinny people looked suspicious to the ancients. (Remember that the back-stabbing Cassius had a "lean and hungry look.") The rise in the BMI from the nineteenth century to about 1960 should be counted as one of the great social and medical victories of modern times. In a sense, it created a more equal social status, as well as a more equal physical stature.

So what went wrong more recently? It is not the case that the average BMI has suddenly accelerated. In fact, the BMI has been rising fairly steadily for the past 120 years. Nonetheless, since the 1960s the higher BMI scores have surpassed the optimal zone of about 20 to 25. No doubt, a more sedentary lifestyle adds to this concern. (In contrast, the healthy rise in BMIs during the early 1900s might be attributed to gaining more muscle, which weighs more than fat.) The post-1960s rise in BMI scores is similar to a tree that grows 12 inches per year but in its tenth year starts casting an unwanted shadow on your patio. In the case of people, more mass from fat has diminishing returns, cutting down their life spans and raising the risk for diabetes, heart disease, gallbladder disease, and even cancer. Over half of American adults are overweight, and nearly a quarter actually qualify as obese, according to the National Institutes of Health.

Should we chiefly blame fast food for BMIs over 25? According to the caricature described by lawyers suing fast food companies, poor, ill-educated people are duped by duplicitous restaurant franchises into biting into greasy hamburgers and french fries. The data, however, tell us that this theory is wrong. If the "blame fast food" hypothesis were correct, we would see a faster pace of BMI growth among poorly educated people, who might not be able to read or understand nutritional labels. In fact, college-educated people—not the poorly educated—accounted for the most rapid growth in BMI scores between the 1970s and the 1990s. (Poorly educated people have a higher overall incidence of obesity.) The percentage of obese college-educated women nearly tripled between the early 1970s and the early 1990s. In comparison, the proportion of obese women without high school degrees rose by only 58 percent. Among men, the results were similar. Obesity among those without high school degrees climbed by about 53 percent, but obesity among college graduates jumped by 163 percent. If the "blame fast food" hypothesis made sense, these data would be flipped upside down.

The Sources of Additional Calories

Of course, we cannot deny that people are eating more and getting bigger, but that does not prove that fast food franchises are the culprit. On average, Americans are eating about 200 calories more each day than they did in the 1970s. . . .

So where are the 200 additional calories coming from? The U.S. Department of Agriculture (USDA) has compiled the "Continuing Survey of Food Intakes by Individuals," which collects information on where a food was purchased, how it was prepared, and where it was eaten, in addition to demographic information such as race, income, age, and sex. The survey shows that the answer is as close as the nearest salty treat. Americans are not eating bigger breakfasts, lunches, or dinners—but they are noshing and nibbling like never before. Between the 1970s and the 1990s, men and women essentially doubled the calories consumed between meals (by between 160 and 240 calories). In 1987–88, Americans typically snacked less than once a day; by 1994 they were snacking 1.6 times per day. But surely, opponents of fast food would argue, those cookies and pre-wrapped apple pies at McDonald's must account for calories. Again the data fail to make their case. Women ate only about six more snack calories at fast food restaurants, while men ate eight more snack calories, over the past two decades. That is roughly equal to one Cheez-It cracker or a few raisins. Where do Americans eat their between-meal calories? Mostly at home. Kitchen cabinets can be deadly to diets. And in a fairly recent development, supermarket shoppers are pulling goodies off of store shelves and ripping into them at the stores before they even drive home. Consumers eat two to three times more goodies inside stores than at fast food restaurants.

Food Is More Affordable

Why are people eating more and growing larger? For one thing, food is cheaper. From an historical point of view that is a very good thing. A smaller portion of today's family budget goes to food than at any time during the twentieth century. In 1929, families spent 23.5 percent of their incomes on food. In 1961, they spent 17 percent. By 2001, American families could

"How to Get Fat in America," cartoon by Larry Wright. *The Detroit News*, 2003. Copyright © 2003. Reproduced by permission of Cagle Cartoons, Inc.

spend just 10 percent of their incomes on food, according to the USDA's Economic Research Service. The lower relative cost of food made it easier, of course, for people to consume more.

Since the mid-1980s we have seen an interesting change in restaurant pricing, which has made restaurants more attractive to consumers. Compared to supermarket prices, restaurant prices have actually fallen since 1986. Whereas a restaurant meal was 1.82 times the cost of a store-bought meal in 1986, by 2001 a restaurant meal cost just 1.73 times as much. Higher incomes and lower relative restaurant prices have induced people to eat more, and to eat more away from home.

Despite the attraction of restaurant eating and the proliferation of sit-down chain restaurants such as the Olive Garden, TGI Friday's, P.F. Chang's, and others, Americans still consume about two-thirds of their calories at home. Critics of fast food spend little time comparing fast food meals to meals eaten at home, at schools, or at sit-down restaurants. . . .

Very few defenders of fast food would tell moms and dads to throw out the home-cooked meal and instead eat 21 meals a week at White Castle. But it is a mistake to stereotype fast food as simply a cheeseburger and a large fries. Fast food restaurants have vastly expanded their menus for a variety of reasons including health concerns and demographic shifts. The increasing role of Hispanic Americans in determining national food tastes has inspired many fast food franchises to offer tacos, burritos, and salsa salads. Wendy's, traditionally known for its square-shaped hamburgers, offers a low-fat chili dish that the Minnesota attorney general's office recommended as a "healthier choice" in its fast food guide. McDonald's has continuously revamped its menu in recent years. On March 10, 2003, the company unveiled a new line of "premium salads" that feature Newman's Own All-Natural Dressings. In its publicity blitz, McDonald's facetiously asked, "What's Next? Wine Tasting?" Meanwhile Burger King features broiled chicken teriyaki in addition to its traditional fare. Judge Sweet noted that the Subway sandwich chain, which boasts of healthy choices, hired a spokesman who apparently lost 230 pounds of weight while eating the "Subway Diet." In fact, fast food meals today derive fewer calories from fat than they did in the 1970s. Consumers can customize their fast food meals, too. Simply by asking for "no mayo," they may cut down fat calories by an enormous proportion. It is worth pointing out that fast food firms introduced these alternative meals in response to changing consumer tastes, not in reply to dubious lawsuits. During the 1990s, McDonald's and Taco Bell invested millions of dollars trying to develop low-fat, commercially viable selections such as the McLean Deluxe hamburger and Taco Bell's Border Lights. Burger King adopted its "Have It Your Way" slogan several decades ago. . . .

Consumers Deserve Choices

Faced with the conundrum of changing tastes and nutritional recommendations, Judge Sweet shrewdly took up the distinction between an inherently dangerous meal and a meal that may pose some legitimate risk, if only from over-consumption. The Restatement (Second) of Torts explained that "Ordinary sugar is a deadly poison to some diabetics" and that "Good whiskey is not unreasonably dangerous merely because it will make some people drunk, and is especially dangerous to alcoholics; but bad whiskey, containing a dangerous amount of fuel oil, is unreasonably dangerous." These risks are not good reasons to outlaw good sugar or good whiskey. Fried fish may be oily, but that does not mean it is contaminated. Absent a truly compelling and sweeping health reason, we should not let lawsuits rob consumers of choices. . . .

Let us be frank here. Depending on what you pile on it, a fast food burger may not enhance your health, and it may even hinder your ability to run a marathon—but it is very easy to find out how fatty that burger is. You do not need a lawyer by your side to pry open a brochure or to check the thousands of websites that will provide nutrition data. While it is unlikely that nutritionists will soon announce that super-sized double cheeseburgers will make you thin, society should not allow the latest fads or the most lucrative lawsuits to govern what we eat for lunch.

> *"The true driver of childhood obesity these days is a steady decline in physical activity."*

A Lack of Physical Activity Causes Obesity

Richard Berman

Sedentary lifestyles, not food advertising, are to blame for childhood obesity, Richard Berman opines in the following viewpoint. He contends that despite the claims of some organizations and politicians, no evidence exists to prove a connection between advertising and food consumption. Rather, Berman argues, children are becoming increasingly obese because they are physically inactive, a problem worsened by schools cutting back on physical education classes. Berman is the executive director for the Center for Consumer Freedom, a nonprofit coalition supported by food companies, consumers, and restaurants.

As you read, consider the following questions:

1. According to Berman, why do politicians blame food advertising for childhood obesity?

2. What proportion of American children get no physical activity, according to the author?

3. As explained by Berman, what happened to Kraft after it took steps to make its products healthier?

Richard Berman, "Sloth, Not Ads, Is Responsible for Fat Kids," *Advertising Age*, Vol. 76, April 18, 2005, p. 30. Copyright © 2005 Crain Communications, Inc. Reproduced by permission.

Everywhere you look, food advertising is being blamed for childhood obesity. The World Health Organization and the Institute of Medicine have hit the industry for its practices. The Federal Trade Commission is getting in the game. And . . . Iowa Sen. Tom Harkin has threatened advertisers and food companies with draconian legislation. Harkin's statements invoke a body of scientific evidence supposedly linking food advertising with childhood obesity. To put it nicely, this is wishful thinking. There is simply no solid evidence of a connection. At the same time, there are many compelling reasons to believe that no relationship exists.

Advertising Does Not Cause Obesity

The vast majority of people believe that parents, not food advertising, represent the primary factor in kids' food choices and weight. And the experts agree. "Despite media claims to the contrary," one . . . article in the *Journal of the Royal Society of Medicine* noted, "there is no good evidence that advertising has a substantial influence on children's food consumption and, consequently, no reason to believe that a complete ban on advertising would have any useful impact on childhood obesity rates." The article pointed out that countries such as Sweden, and provinces such as Canada's Quebec, have banned food advertising to kids, and they're no thinner than the rest of us.

Even the inventor of punitive "fat taxes" (also known as the "Twinkie tax"), Yale University Professor Kelly Brownell admits: "There is only circumstantial evidence that the ads cause poor eating." The "circumstantial" evidence generally cited by anti-advertising crusaders relates to a moderate correlation between TV viewing and childhood obesity. Of course, the fact that watching TV is a sedentary behavior in itself is rarely mentioned. Nor do industry opponents like to admit that the connection between obesity and video games (where

Physical Activity and Health

- Physical activity tops the list of Leading Health Indicators (LHI) in Healthy People 2010, the government's published health goals and objectives for the next decade.

- Poor diet and inactivity can lead to overweight/obesity. Persons who are overweight or obese are at increased risk for high blood pressure, type 2 diabetes, coronary heart disease, stroke, gallbladder disease, osteoarthritis, sleep apnea, respiratory problems and some types of cancer.

- The major barriers most people face when trying to increase physical activity are time, access to convenient facilities, and safe environments in which to be active.

- School-based and workplace based interventions have been shown to be successful in increasing physical activity levels.

- Physical activity among children and adolescents is important because of the related health benefits (cardio-respiratory function, blood pressure control, weight management, cognitive and emotional benefits).

President's Council on Physical Fitness and Sports,
"Facts and Resources on the Health Benefits of
Physical Activity," 2005.

food advertising is rare) is much stronger than the connection between obesity and TV viewing.

Physical Inactivity Is to Blame

It's easy for politicians to blame food advertising. That's because regulating it doesn't cost any money. But the true driver of childhood obesity these days is a steady decline in physical activity—and addressing that problem will require serious tradeoffs.

"In a debate that has often focused on foods alone," former Food and Drug Commissioner Dr. Mark McClellan observes, "actual levels of caloric intake among the young haven't appreciably changed over the last 20 years." Unlike Mr. Harkin's claims about food advertising, a growing body of research does indeed corroborate McClellan's point.

Earlier [in 2005], research published in the *Archives of Pediatrics and Adolescent Medicine* found "insufficient vigorous physical activity was the only risk factor" for overweight children. An article in the *American Journal of Clinical Nutrition* noted: "The lack of evidence of a general increase in energy intake among youths despite an increase in the prevalence of overweight suggests that physical inactivity is a major public health challenge in this age group." And an article in the *Journal of Clinical Endocrinology & Metabolism* pointed out: "It is often assumed that the increase in pediatric obesity has occurred because of an increase in caloric intake. However, the data do not substantiate this."

Schools Are Cutting Back on Physical Education

All of this makes intuitive sense. If Grandpa hiked three miles in the snow (uphill both ways, of course) to get to school, and Dad traveled to junior high on his bike, today's kids get door-to-door service in the family minivan. Walking and biking trips made by children have dropped more than 60% since the late 1970s. A full quarter of American children get no physical activity whatsoever.

Schools have become part of the problem. With tight budgets and a renewed focus on reading and math, gym is going the way of the dinosaurs. An article in the journal *Pediatrics* found that only 21% of American adolescents participate in a physical education class each week. Meanwhile, food is getting a bum rap. It may sound counterintuitive, but after studying more than 14,000 American children, a team of six Harvard doctors found that snack food and soda do not contribute to childhood obesity. The study, which was published in the *International Journal of Obesity*, concluded: "Our data did not offer support for the hypothesis that snacking promotes weight gain."

As is often the case in emotionally charged debates, policy is getting far ahead of research. The self-described "food police" at the Center for Science in the Public Interest [CSPI] have urged litigation by trial lawyers and state attorneys general to restrict food advertising to children. A government commission in Maine recently proposed extra taxes on advertising certain foods to kids. And—*sacre bleu!*—France has already enacted such a proposal.

The Danger of Making Concessions

The science may not be on their side, but industry opponents have the momentum. Defending food advertising in this environment has certain risks. Nevertheless, the risks associated with giving in to political pressure are even greater.

Consider what happened to Kraft after its 2003 announcement that it would reduce sugar, fat and calories in many of its products, shrink single-serve portions and limit marketing to children. Far from getting credit from trial lawyers and the food police, Kraft was subjected to further demands and increased scrutiny. CSPI called Kraft's moves just a first step and insisted on further restrictions. Obesity lawsuit instigator John Banzhaf informed *BusinessWeek* that he still intended to litigate based on the company's child-oriented marketing. And Banzhaf's colleagues at the Public Health Advocacy Institute [PHAI] sent a letter threatening legal action against Kraft unless the company could prove its customers were actually getting thinner.

"Kraft's policy suggests marketing high calorie-density products to kids is improper and perhaps substantially harmful," argues law professor, tobacco lawsuit veteran, and PHAI board member Richard Daynard. Wharton marketing professor Patti Williams echoes Daynard, saying: "A company that pulls the plug on its advertising to children is acknowledging there is something wrong with that advertising."

Williams and Daynard have a point. Whether in the courtroom, or the court of public opinion, voluntarily limiting food advertising to children looks like an implicit admission of guilt. As a result, compromise would be self-defeating. Better to spend more money promoting the real evidence rather than making concessions to those who will continuously and incrementally move the goalposts.

> *"Economic factors do seem to influence behaviors that may lead to weight differences among individuals."*

Economic Factors Contribute to Obesity

Lisa Mancino, Biing-Hwan Lin, and Nicole Ballenger

In the following viewpoint Lisa Mancino, Biing-Hwan Lin, and Nicole Ballenger assert that economic factors such as income and the price of foods can determine whether people become obese. They contend that while people with higher incomes may be able to afford a healthier diet, these wealthier people may also gain weight if they spend more time working and less time exercising. At the other end of the income scale, poor people often live in neighborhoods with few parks and trails; thus the poor often exercise little and become obese. Mancino is an agricultural economist and Lin is a senior economist at the U.S. Department of Agriculture's Economic Research Service. Ballenger is a professor and the head of the department of agricultural and applied economics at the University of Wyoming in Laramie.

As you read, consider the following questions:

1. According to the authors, what proportion of obese adolescents become obese adults?
2. What is an individual's full income, as defined by the authors?

Lisa Mancino, Biing-Hwan Lin, and Nicole Ballenger, "The Role of Economics in Eating Choices and Weight Outcomes," *Agriculture Information Bulletin*, no. 791, September 2004.

3. In the view of the authors, why are single parents likely to gain weight?

Obesity rates among adult Americans have doubled within the past 25 years. In 1999–2000, nearly 65 percent of U.S. adults were either overweight or obese. Obesity accounts for $117 billion a year in direct and indirect economic costs, it is associated with 300,000 deaths each year, and it will soon overtake tobacco as the leading cause of preventable deaths. Magnifying the public cost, Medicaid and Medicare were estimated to have paid for over half of all U.S. medical expenses related to overweight and obesity in 1998.

The risk of being overweight has been increasing among children as well. Over 15 percent of children age 6 to 19 are either overweight or at risk of becoming overweight, according to recent estimates. For children age 6–12, this represents a 135-percent increase from 1976. For children age 12–19, the increase is 210 percent. For an adolescent, the probability of childhood obesity persisting into adulthood is as high as 80 percent. So the trends in overweight and obesity are likely to continue if left unchecked.

An Unequal Risk

The incidence of obesity has risen across America and among all population groups. Not everyone, however, is equally at risk of becoming overweight or obese, or at risk for the same reasons. . . . Understanding weight differences and predispositions to obesity is one approach to finding solutions. Understanding differences in risk can be used to tailor education and intervention campaigns and more efficiently allocate funds.

One determinant of body weight is a person's genetic makeup. Medical studies have shown that genetic differences explain a significant amount of weight variation both among individuals and over time for a given individual. However, much of the variation in body weight is also related to behavior: what we eat and how active we are. This is cause for hope because behaviors are amenable to change. Our first objective is to see if we can link specific eating and physical activity behaviors—as well as knowledge, attitudes, and perceptions that affect such behaviors—with weight outcomes.

To promote specific behavioral changes, we need to understand the motivation behind these behaviors. Economic analysis is suited to this task because it helps explain how individuals choose to allocate their limited resources—including their time and money—to eating a healthful diet, engaging in physical activity, and being informed about diet, health, and weight relationships. More important, are economic factors (costs, income, etc.) behind differences in behaviors and attitudes that affect weight outcomes? . . .

Key Economic Factors

We developed an economic framework to determine if and how economic factors might explain differences in the behaviors and attitudes that we found to be correlated with weight outcomes. This framework is based on the biological relationship between calories consumed and calories expended, where excess body weight results when someone routinely consumes more calories than he or she expends. How many calories we choose to consume and how many calories we expend daily are influenced by a constellation of factors. . . . Each factor may play a multifaceted role, affecting an individual's knowledge about health and nutrition, his or her choice of what to eat, and how many calories he or she expends.

Prices. Economic theory assumes that relative differences in prices can partially explain differences among individuals in terms of their food choices, leisure activities, and knowledge about diet and health. For example, avocados may cost less in California than in Minnesota. If buyers of avocados were alike in every other way, we would expect the Californian to purchase more avocados than the Minnesotan. We may also expect relative differences in the price or accessibility of information to shape an individual's knowledge and attitudes about diet and health. Public health campaigns, which reduce the price of information, tend to focus on areas or populations that are most at risk of coming in contact with a specific health threat. For example, Texans may have different attitudes and knowledge about how to avoid West Nile virus than people in Montana. Economic theory also assumes that the full price of a good or service includes its monetary price as well as other costs, such as travel costs and time. Thus, an individual living near a public park may choose to be more active than someone else living in an area with few walking trails, sidewalks, or bike trails.

Full Income. An individual's full income is the fusion of the amount of money, time, and ability he or she has to either purchase or produce goods and services. For example, someone may allocate his or her time, money, and ability to painting the exterior of his or her house, or may hire a contractor to do the job. The choice depends on the price the contractor charges versus the price of materials, on the time needed to paint the exterior (which is related to painting skills), and on what else this person could be doing (opportunity costs).

Economic theory uses the concept of full income to explain differences in choices regarding food and physical activity. For example, as individuals' wages increase, their incomes increase and they have more money to spend on everything: food, other goods, and leisure activities. Wage increases also inflate the value of their time because time spent working has increased in value relative to time spent in leisure or working around the house. This change may compel individuals to purchase goods and services that are more convenient, more prepared, or higher quality. An increase in wage rates also raises the full cost of ill health, which includes the cost of medical treatment needed to regain health and time lost work-

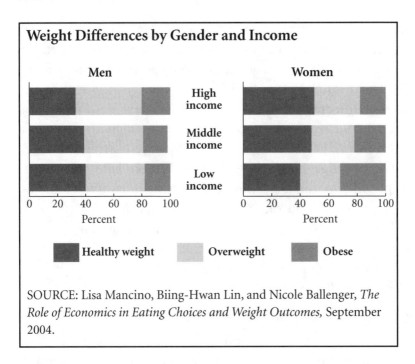

Weight Differences by Gender and Income

SOURCE: Lisa Mancino, Biing-Hwan Lin, and Nicole Ballenger, *The Role of Economics in Eating Choices and Weight Outcomes,* September 2004.

ing. As such, individuals with higher incomes should have more incentives to invest in their own health. They may choose to make these investments by eating more healthfully and engaging in more active pursuits.

Allocating Time and Money

However, there are opposing forces that may compel individuals to gain weight as income increases. As time spent working in the market becomes more valuable, an individual may devote more time to such work by spending less time at leisure. With sedentary work, this reallocation of time will lead to fewer calories expended. If this is not offset by a reduction in calories consumed, then an individual will likely gain weight. As time spent working in the market becomes more valuable, an individual may also choose to purchase foods that are more prepared. If these foods are higher in calories, or if that individual is less aware of the caloric and nutrient content of these purchased foods, weight gain is again likely.

Other factors related to time allocation may affect how individuals choose which foods to buy and how much to exercise. For one, the extra costs incurred from poor nutrition should be at least as high for individuals with children as for individuals with no children. However, the extra costs of preparing food may actually be lower for individuals with children. The time costs to prepare a meal for two people are not much different than to prepare a meal for four. Also, many food manufacturers offer volume discounts. Thus, as individuals prepare food for more people, the relative time and monetary costs decline, while the extra benefits of preparing a healthful meal remain at least as high. Therefore, economic theory predicts that, all else equal, an individual with children is more likely to make healthful food choices than an individual without children.

Opposing forces are at work here too. Some factors may compel individuals to gain weight as family size increases. This is more likely for single parents who are responsible for both providing the family income and tending to housework. As these individuals devote more time to working and tending to household chores, they will have less time for active pursuits. They may also choose to purchase foods that are more prepared. If these time substitutions lead to fewer calories expended or less awareness of the caloric and nutrient content of foods eaten, weight gain is again likely. . . .

Correlation Between Incomes and Healthy Behavior

Economic theory suggests that demand for goods and services used to maintain or improve one's health increases with income. We used the household's Poverty Income Ratio (PIR) to group individuals into three different income categories: low, middle, and high. The PIR is the ratio of a household's income to the Federal poverty guideline for that household's number of family members. In this study, a household was considered to be low income if its PIR fell below 185 percent of the Federal poverty level. Households above 185 percent typically do not qualify for most social programs, such as Head Start, the Food Stamp Program, the National School Lunch Program, and the Children's Health Insurance Program. An individual whose household income fell between 185 and 300 percent of the poverty level was classified as middle income. Individuals with household incomes that exceeded 300 percent of the poverty level were classified as high income.

Our empirical results show that income and healthy weight behaviors are correlated in the following ways:

- Compared with all other explanatory variables, income had the strongest marginal impact on diet quality and the amount of time spent watching TV. Both men and women with higher incomes watch less TV and eat a higher quality diet.

- Women with higher incomes drink fewer sugary beverages, such as fruit drinks and soft drinks, and have a higher sense of self-efficacy regarding weight control. Also, a higher proportion of women with higher incomes indicate that they exercise at least once a week.

- Men with higher incomes are more accurate in reporting their weight status. . . .

It would be misleading to suggest that weight differences are entirely the result of personal choices. It would also be naive to suggest that personal choices are entirely shaped by the economic variables we considered. However, economic factors do seem to influence behaviors that may lead to weight differences among individuals.

| *"Schools are serving kids the very foods that lead to obesity, diabetes, and heart disease."*

School Lunches Cause Childhood Obesity

Barry Yeoman

Schools are partly to blame for childhood obesity because of the high-fat, high-calorie foods they serve, Barry Yeoman maintains in the following viewpoint. According to Yeoman, the National School Lunch Program was established to make healthy meals affordable for all students, but in fact its ultimate effect is to provide schools with meat and dairy products. Yeoman argues that by relying primarily on these high-fat foods to prepare their meals, schools are contributing to the high rate of obesity among adolescents. Yeoman is a frequent contributor to the bimonthly magazine Mother Jones.

As you read, consider the following questions:

1. How much money does the U.S. government spend on farm products under the National School Lunch Program, according to Yeoman?

2. As stated by Yeoman, the obesity rates of adolescents have increased by what amount since 1980?

3. What percentage of public high schools sells fast food in their cafeterias, according to the author?

Every weekday at lunch, courtesy of the federal government, more than 27 million schoolchildren sit down to the nation's largest mass feeding. If we took a giant snapshot of their trays on a typical day—say, Tuesday, September 24 [2002]—here's what the continent-wide photo would look like:

In Lynnwood, Washington, we would see kids eating sausage with Belgian waffle sticks and syrup. In Clovis, California, bacon cheeseburgers. In La Quinta, California, Canadian bacon and cheese rolls. In Rexburg, Idaho, cheese nachos and waffles. In Fort Collins, Colorado, "homemade" pigs in a blanket. In Bryan, Texas, cheeseburgers, chicken-fried steak, and pizza. In Hot Springs, Arkansas, country steak with creamed potatoes. In Cedar Falls, Iowa, mini-corndogs. In Lafayette, Indiana, beef ravioli with cheesy broccoli. In Columbus, Ohio, egg rolls with tater tots. In Kingstree, South Carolina, sloppy joes with onion rings. In Richmond, Virginia, chili cheese nachos. In Gatesville, North Carolina, three-meat subs with Fritos. In Orwigsburg, Pennsylvania, cheese steak on rolls with buttered pasta. And in Fitchburg, Massachusetts, pretzels with cheese sauce.

Here and there, we'd also see baked chicken and salads. But by and large, school cafeterias coast to coast offer an artery-clogging menu of beef, pork, cheese, and grease. "Whenever I see children clinically, I ask them if they buy lunch at school or bring it from home," says Patricia Froberg, a nutritionist at Connecticut Children's Medical Center in Hartford. "If they say, 'I get it at school,' I cringe."

Conflicting Goals

At a time when weight-related illnesses in children are escalating, schools are serving kids the very foods that lead to obesity, diabetes, and heart disease. That's because the National School Lunch Program, which gives schools more than $6 billion each year to offer low-cost meals to students, has conflicting missions. Enacted in 1946, the program is supposed to provide healthy meals to children, regardless of income. At the same time, however, it's designed to subsidize agribusiness, shoring up demand for beef and milk even as the public's taste for these foods declines.

Under the program, the federal government buys up more than $800 million worth of farm products each year and turns them over to schools to serve their students. The U.S. Department of Agriculture [USDA], which administers the system, calls this a win-win situation: Schools get free ingredients while farmers are guaranteed a steady income. The trouble is, most of the commodities provided to schools are meat and dairy products, often laden with saturated fat. In 2001, the USDA spent a total of $350 million on surplus beef and cheese for schools—more than double the $161 million spent on all fruits and vegetables, most of which were canned or frozen. On top of its regular purchases, the USDA makes special purchases in direct response to industry lobbying. In November 2001, for example, the beef industry wrote to Agriculture Secretary Ann Veneman, complaining that a decline in travel after [the September 11, 2001, terrorist attacks], along with a lowered demand for beef in Japan, was suppressing sales of their product. The department responded two months later with a $30 million "bonus buy" of frozen beef roasts and ground beef for schools.

"Basically, it's a welfare program for suppliers of commodities," says Jennifer Raymond, a retired nutritionist in Northern California who has worked with schools to develop healthier menus. "It's a price support program for agricultural producers, and the schools are simply a way to get rid of the items that have been purchased."

All in all, schools obtain almost 20 percent of their food from the commodities program—and they depend on the handouts to meet tight budgets. "School districts are under intense budgetary pressure, and oftentimes nutrition is at the bottom of the priority list," says David Ludwig, director of the obesity program at Children's Hospital in Boston. School nutrition directors face increasing mandates from their higher-ups to break even, or even make a profit, and therefore have no choice but to accept surplus commodities. "They help shape our menus significantly, especially if you're going to run a program successfully financially," says Christy Koury, director of child nutrition for schools in Freeport, Texas, where menus run heavy on hamburgers, cheese-stuffed pizza sticks, and pepperoni calzones.

School nutrition officials like Koury consider the free food so vital to their budgets that they have sometimes overlooked good nutrition to side with the beef and dairy industries, forming a powerful alliance that has blocked efforts to serve healthier meals to students. The National School Lunch Program is up for reauthorization this year [2003] [reauthorization occurred] for the first time since 1998, but given the interests backing the current system, few expect Congress to approve any meaningful reforms. "It's understood that commodity programs exist," says Graydon Forrer, former director of consumer affairs for the USDA, "and that commodity programs will continue to exist." . . .

High Fat Levels

School boards, coping with tight budgets, aren't willing to spend more for better nutrition. Huntsville [Alabama], for example, left 50 teaching slots empty this year to trim its $187 million budget. "The school food service is held hostage, because they can't go into the open market and buy healthy foods and stay profitable," says Raymond, the retired nutritionist.

Schools rely on the commodities program for another reason: It fits neatly into the decades-old method they have traditionally used to prepare school meals. Known as "food-based menu planning," the system mandates specific servings of meat, dairy, vegetable, and grain on each child's plate—without bothering to determine the meal's total nutritional value. "It's been done that way for so long," says Suzanne Havala Hobbs, a former spokeswoman for the American Dietetic Association who teaches nutrition at the University of North Carolina. "There's just resistance to change."

The USDA insists that school lunches are getting healthier. "There have been tremendous moves to reduce the fat content in school meals," says department spokeswoman Jean Daniel. In recent years, the government has lowered the acceptable fat levels for ground beef and pork, introduced light cheeses and ground turkey, and eliminated tropical oils from its peanut butter.

For the most part, though, fat levels remain dangerously high. Based on USDA recommendations, an adolescent girl who eats a 730-calorie lunch should receive no more than 24 grams of fat, and no more than 8 grams of saturated fat. Yet one portion of USDA surplus chuck roast, plus a glass of whole milk, delivers 31 grams of fat, including 14 grams of saturated fat. Buttered rolls and a side dish of cheesy broccoli bump those figures even higher. And if a school wants to cut animal fat by eliminating whole milk, it can't: Federal law requires that schools continue offering it as long as 1 percent of the students purchase it. As a result, school lunches routinely fail the government's own nutritional standards. By law, schools are supposed to restrict fat content in lunches to 30 percent of the calories served each week. But according to the USDA, 81 percent of schools exceed that limit. Worse, 85 percent fail the standard for saturated fat, a leading contributor to coronary disease. Half of all schools serve whole milk, which further drives up the saturated-fat content. On any

"Why Yes, I have heard the old saying . . . ," cartoon by Farrington. Cagle Cartoons. Reproduced by permission of Cagle Cartoons.

given day, less than 45 percent of schools serve cooked vegetables other than potatoes—which are often prepared in the form of french fries—and less than 10 percent serve legumes, a healthy, low-fat form of protein.

A Growing Health Crisis

School food directors say they have to serve fatty meals to satisfy the tastes of children raised on McDonald's and Domino's. "They'd love to have pizza and french fries every day," says [Carol] Wheelock, the Huntsville official. "You can't eliminate French fries." Adding fat is sometimes the only way to get kids to eat green vegetables. "A little bit of cheese on broccoli they love," she says. "The benefit from eating the broccoli will far outweigh a little additional fat." But all that cheese adds up. Public schools serve more than 4 billion meals every year—a number that would make many fast-food chains envious—

and officials say all those lunches are contributing to the growing health crisis among kids. According to the Centers for Disease Control and Prevention, obesity rates have doubled in children and tripled in adolescents since 1980, spurring an epidemic of type II diabetes, once considered an adult-onset condition. Obesity has also been associated with heart disease, arthritis, and certain cancers, and researchers have found fatty streaks in the blood vessels of children as young as 10.

"USDA needs to relate the current crisis in kids' health to the meals that are being served, especially to poor kids, because that's the population that's most vulnerable," says Antonia Demas, director of the Food Studies Institute, a child-nutrition group based in upstate New York. Because low-income children often eat both breakfast and lunch at school, "they get at least two-thirds of their calories from school each day, and they're the population really showing an increase in the diet-related diseases." . . .

Taking a New Approach

Although Congress did set fat limits for school lunches, it created no effective mechanism for reaching those standards—and no penalty for failing. "It was a baby step forward, but our problems are so drastic that far greater changes are needed before we see a substantial improvement in kids' health," says dietitian Havala Hobbs. Even [Marshall] Matz, a food-service lobbyist, regrets the battle. "Good God, we spent two years arguing about process," he says. "Those years were a lost opportunity."

[In 2003], Congress will take up the National School Lunch Program for the first time in five years.[1] But industry representatives and health experts agree there will be no serious effort to prevent schools from serving children so many cheeseburgers, pizzas, and french fries. Instead, most of the debate

1. Congress reauthorized the program and added a requirement that school districts who participate in NSLP must enact wellness policies by the beginning of the 2006–07 school year.

is expected to center on who serves up those items. The food-service association estimates that 30 percent of all public high schools currently sell Burger King, Domino's Pizza, and other brand-name fast food in their cafeterias alongside federally subsidized meals, and many more dispense chips and sodas in vending machines down the hall. Nutrition experts want the USDA to regulate corporate vendors in schools, but such "competitive" foods appeal to cash-strapped districts, many of which are eager to accept money from fast-food companies to open franchises right on campus.

The debate over fast food is sure to grab headlines, but nutrition advocates warn that it will do nothing to improve the unhealthy meals currently served to the nation's children every weekday. "If Johnny can't read by first grade, parents are going to be up in arms," says Connie Holt, a dietitian who teaches at Widener University in Pennsylvania. "But if he gains five pounds in first grade and doesn't eat well, nobody's going to say anything. All of the health problems we're seeing in the adult world, we have an opportunity to make a difference—but only if we approach school lunch differently."

Periodical Bibliography

Arne Astrup — "Super-Sized and Diabetic by Frequent Fast-Food Consumption?" *Lancet*, January 1, 2005.

Doug Bandow — "It Ain't My Fault," *Chronicles*, September 2003.

Marie Cocco — "U.S. Action Can Help Curb Obesity," *Liberal Opinion Week*, March 29, 2004.

Ron Haskins — "The School Lunch Lobby," *Education Next*, Summer 2005.

Issues and Controversies On File — "Obesity," April 9, 2004.

Patrick Johnson — "Obesity: Epidemic or Myth?" *Skeptical Inquirer*, September/October 2005.

Cynthia Lynn-Garbe — "Weighing in on the Issue of Childhood Obesity," *Childhood Education*, Winter 2004/2005.

Cathy Newman — "Why Are We So Fat?" *National Geographic*, August 2004.

Gary Ruskin — "The Fast Food Trap," *Mothering*, November/December 2003.

Janet Shortt — "Obesity—a Public Health Dilemma," *AORN Journal*, December 2004.

Peg Tyre and Sarah Staveley-O'Carroll — "How to Fix School Lunch," *Newsweek*, August 8, 2005.

Robert E. Wright — "It Just Ain't So!" *Ideas on Liberty*, April 2003.

OPPOSING
VIEWPOINTS®
SERIES

CHAPTER 4

How Can Hunger Be Reduced?

Chapter Preface

Throughout history people have looked to technology to improve agricultural practices and thus reduce world hunger. Many analysts claim that the most successful application of agricultural technology was the "Green Revolution." In the 1960s scientists and researchers developed improved strains of wheat, rice, and other grains that led to increased crop yields in Mexico and Asia. Agricultural methods such as the use of pesticides and chemical fertilizers were also introduced to developing nations. This Green Revolution has been credited with saving more than 1 billion people from starvation. Its leader, Norman Borlaug, was awarded the 1970 Nobel Peace Prize. However, more than three decades later, debate persists on whether the Green Revolution was successful.

Critics of the revolution acknowledge that these new crops and methods led to increased production, but they argue that technology cannot address the larger issues surrounding hunger. Peter Rosset, the former executive director of the Institute for Food and Development Policy, writes, "Narrowly focusing on increasing production—as the Green Revolution does—cannot alleviate hunger because it fails to alter the tightly concentrated distribution of economic power, especially access to land and purchasing power." According to Rosset, poor farmers typically cannot afford fertilizer and are often unable to obtain sufficient water, thus making it harder for their farmland to thrive. Rosset also notes that despite the increased food supply, hunger still persists because the poor cannot afford to buy food.

The effects of the Green Revolution on the environment, in particular on farmland, are also a concern of both its supporters and opponents. The McKnight Foundation, an organization that funds nonprofit programs, including research relating to food security, praises the results of the revolution. In particular, it notes that China has been able to feed its growing population while using less land. However, the foundation acknowledges, "The combination of fertilizers, pesticides, and enhanced seeds caused ecological problems, including pesticide poisoning, in some parts of the world." Rosset points out that the technologies introduced by the revolution appear to be backfiring; yields are declining and soil is degrading in quality. He writes, "Years of using high-yield seeds that require heavy irrigation and chemical fertilizers have taken their toll on much of India's farmland. So far, 6 percent of agricultural land has been rendered useless."

These criticisms suggest that the Green Revolution may have had only limited success at reducing hunger. With so many factors contributing to hunger, such as poverty and access to healthy foods, it is unlikely that technology will ever solve world hunger. In the following chapter the authors debate various approaches to fighting hunger. Governments, businesses, nonprofit organizations, and private citizens will all likely need to contribute if worldwide hunger is to be significantly reduced.

> "[The Food and Nutrition Service's] mission is to increase food security, reduce hunger and improve health outcomes."

Government Programs Help Reduce Hunger

Roberto Salazar

In the following viewpoint Roberto Salazar, the administrator of the Food and Nutrition Service [FNS], a government agency that manages fifteen nutrition assistance programs, explains the steps the federal government is taking to reduce hunger in America. According to Salazar, programs such as the National School Lunch Program and the Food Stamp Program enable millions of Americans to eat a nutritious diet. In addition he asserts that in order for these programs to remain effective, improper payments must be reduced, the government needs to continue to work with faith-based organizations, and the FNS must make its workforce more effective. This viewpoint was originally delivered as testimony before the Senate Subcommittee on Agriculture, Rural Development, and Related Agencies.

As you read, consider the following questions:

1. What proportion of Americans use federal nutrition assistance programs, according to Salazar?

Roberto Salazar, "Food and Nutrition Service Statement before the Senate Subcommittee on Agriculture, Rural Development, and Related Agencies," April 14, 2005.

2. What steps does Salazar say the Food and Nutrition Service will take to minimize improper program payments?

3. According to the author, what serious challenge must be addressed by the FNS?

The Food and Nutrition Service [FNS] is the agency charged with managing fifteen nutrition assistance programs which create the Nation's nutrition safety net and providing Federal leadership in America's ongoing struggle against hunger and poor nutrition. Our stated mission is to increase food security, reduce hunger and improve health outcomes in partnership with cooperating organizations by providing children and low-income people access to nutritious food and nutrition education in a manner that inspires public confidence and supports American agriculture. The budget request clearly demonstrates the President's continuing commitment to this mission and our programs.

Critical Programs

A request of $59 billion in new budget authority is contained within the fiscal year 2006 budget to fulfill this mission through the fifteen FNS nutrition assistance programs. These critical programs touch the lives of more than 1 in 5 Americans over the course of a year. Programs funded within this budget request include the National School Lunch Program (NSLP), which will provide nutritious school lunches to almost 30 million children each school day, the WIC [Women, Infants, and Children] Program, which will assist with the nutrition and health care needs of 8.5 million at-risk pregnant and postpartum women, infants and children each month, and the Food Stamp Program (FSP), which will ensure access to a nutritious diet each month for an estimated 29.1 million people. The remaining programs include the School Breakfast Program (SBP), The Emergency Food Assistance Program (TEFAP), the Summer Food Service Program (SFSP), the

Child and Adult Care Food Program (CACFP), the Food Distribution Program on Indian Reservations (FDPIR), and the Commodity Supplemental Food Program (CSFP) and the Farmers' Market Programs. FNS seeks to serve the children and low-income households of this Nation and address the diverse circumstances through which hunger and nutrition-related problems present themselves and affect our participants within the design and delivery methods of our programs.

The resources we are here to discuss represent an investment in the health, self-sufficiency, and productivity of Americans who, at times, find themselves in need of nutrition assistance. Under Secretary [Eric M.] Bost ... has outlined the three critical challenges which the Food, Nutrition and Consumer Services team has focused on under his leadership: expanding access to the Federal nutrition assistance programs; addressing the growing epidemic of overweight and obesity; and, improving the integrity with which our programs are administered. In addition to these fundamental priorities specific to our mission, the President's Management Agenda provides an ambitious agenda for management improvement across the Federal Government as a whole. I would like to report on our efforts to address three specific items under this agenda; reducing improper payments and enhancing the efficiency of program delivery, building partnerships with faith and community based organizations, and systematically planning for the human capital challenges facing all of the Federal service.

Ensuring Integrity

Good financial management is at the center of the President's Management Agenda. As with any Federal program, the nutrition assistance programs require sustained attention to program integrity. We cannot sustain these programs over the long term without continued public trust in our ability to manage them effectively. Program integrity is as fundamental to our mission as program access or healthy eating. Our efforts to minimize improper program payments focus on 1) working closely with States to improve Food Stamp payment accuracy; 2) implementing policy changes and new oversight efforts to improve school meals certification; and 3) improving management of Child and Adult Care Food Program providers and vendors in WIC. We have identified these 4 programs as programs susceptible to significant improper payments and will continue to enhance the efficiency and accuracy with which these programs are delivered.

I am happy to report that in fiscal year 2003, the most recent year for which data is available, we have achieved a record level of Food Stamp payment accuracy with a combined payment error rate of only 6.63 percent. This is the fifth consecutive year of improvement, making it the lowest rate in the history of the program. With this budget request, we will continue our efforts with our State partners toward continued improvement in the payment error rate. We will continue efforts to address the issue of proper certification in the school meals programs in a way that improves the accuracy of this process without limiting access of eligible children. New analytical work will begin under this budget request to better assess the accuracy of eligibility determinations in the Child and Adult Care Food Program.

Faith-Based and Government Leadership

Faith-based organizations have long played an important role in raising community awareness about program services, assisting individuals who apply for benefits, and delivering benefits. President [George W.] Bush has made working with the faith-based community an Administration priority, and we intend to continue our outreach efforts in FY 2006. The partnership of faith-based organizations and FNS programs, including TEFAP, WIC, NSLP, and the CSFP, is long-established. Most faith-based schools participate in the NSLP and many

Age of Food Stamp Recipients

Participant Characteristic	Total Participants	
	Number	Percent
Children	11,797	50.2
Preschool Age	3,967	16.9
0–1	1,550	6.6
2–4	2,417	10.3
School Age	7,830	33.3
5–7	2,095	8.9
8–11	2,589	11.0
12–15	2,275	9.7
16–17	871	3.7
Nonelderly Adults (18–59)	9,765	41.6
Elderly Adults (60+)	1,919	8.2
Unknown Age	4	0.0

SOURCE: U.S. Department of Agriculture Food and Nutrition Service, *Characteristics of Food Stamp Households: Fiscal Year 2004,* September 2005.

child care providers and sponsors are the product of faith-based organizations. In addition, the majority of organizations such as food pantries and soup kitchens that actually deliver TEFAP benefits are faith-based. Across the country, faith-based organizations have found over the years that they can participate in these programs without compromising their mission or values. They are valued partners in an effort to combat hunger in America. I am happy to report that in the past 6 months we have provided 16 grant awards of approximately $2 million to community and faith-based organizations to test innovative food stamp outreach strategies to reach underserved, eligible individuals and families.

We currently estimate that up to 80 percent of our senior leaders are eligible to retire within five years, as is nearly 30 percent of our total workforce. FNS must address this serious challenge by improving the management of the agency's human capital, strengthening services provided to employees, and implementing programs designed to improve the efficiency, diversity, and competency of the work force. With just nominal increases for basic program administration in most years, the Food and Nutrition Service has reduced its Federal staffing levels significantly over time. We have compensated for these changes by building strong partnerships with the State and local entities which administer our programs and taking advantage of technological innovations. We are extremely proud of what we have accomplished; full funding of the nutrition programs administration request in this budget is vital to our continued success.

"Today it's hard to find a champion for the hungry in Congress, much less in the executive branch."

Government Programs Do Not Help Reduce Hunger

Trudy Lieberman

In the following viewpoint Trudy Lieberman argues that politicians have become indifferent to the needs of America's hungry and have made it increasingly difficult for the poor to receive nutrition assistance. According to Lieberman, the federal government has drastically reduced funding for domestic food programs, while state governments discourage participation in food stamp programs. She contends that cutbacks are likely to continue, particularly because the hungry have no politicians championing their cause. Lieberman is a regular contributor to the magazine Nation.

As you read, consider the following questions:

1. According to the author, how many Americans suffer from food insecurity?

2. How much money did the federal government spend on domestic food programs in 2002, according to Lieberman?

3. In Lieberman's view, what is the only way to achieve self-sufficiency?

Ellen Spearman lives in a trailer at the edge of Morrill, Nebraska, a tiny dusty town near the Wyoming state line. A few years ago she was a member of the working poor, earning $9.10 an hour at a local energy company. Then she got sick and had four surgeries for what turned out to be a benign facial tumor. New owners took over the company and told her she was a medical liability and could not work full time with benefits. For a while she worked part time without benefits until the company eliminated her position. So the 49-year-old single mother of five, with two teenage boys still at home, now lives on $21,300 a year from Social Security disability, child support and payments from the company's long-term disability policy she got as a benefit when she was first hired. That's about $6,000 above the federal poverty level, and too high to qualify for food stamps. But it is not enough to feed her family.

Food Insecurity Is Increasing

Food is the expendable item in a poor person's budget. With the need to pay for gasoline, car insurance, trailer rent, clothes, medicine and utilities, and to make payments on a car loan and $10,000 in medical bills, Spearman says three meals a day "take a back seat." She says she and her family eat a lot of rice with biscuits and gravy. Their diet is more interesting only when a local supermarket sells eight pieces of chicken for $3.99 or chuck roast for $1.49 a pound. "This country doesn't want to admit there's poverty," she says. "We can feed the world but not our own."

Spearman's predicament mirrors that of many Americans. While the most severe forms of malnutrition and starvation that prevailed through the 1960s have largely disappeared, some 33 million people live in households that aren't sure where their next meals are coming from—those whom policy analysts call the food insecure. And with poverty on the rise—the United States experienced the biggest jump in poverty in a decade in 2001, to nearly 12 percent of the population—their ranks are growing. At the end of 2002 the US Conference of Mayors reported a 19 percent increase in the demand for emergency food over the previous year. Food pantries, shelters, soup kitchens and other emergency food providers now serve at least 23 million people a year. "They are America's dirty little secret," says Larry Brown, who directs Brandeis University's Center on Hunger and Poverty. "They are hardworking have-nots who cannot pay the rent, medical bills, and still feed their families."

Food and hunger are a lens through which we see what America has become: a country indifferent to the basic needs of its citizens, one that forces millions of them to rely on private charity that is inadequate, inefficient and frequently unavailable. As people with low and middle incomes have lost their jobs, their families line up for handouts, something many thought they'd never have to do. Hunger exposes the casualties of the ever-widening income gap between the rich and the rest of the population, and the damage inflicted by a twenty-year campaign waged by right-wing think tanks and conservative politicians to defund and delegitimize government. That campaign, which has succeeded in returning the public's view of poverty to the Darwinian one that prevailed before the Progressive Era at the turn of the twentieth century, is emblematic of the right's assault on public programs, which has used the old-fashioned notion of personal failing as the vehicle for accomplishing its political goals. Indeed, few politicians now advocate for the hungry. . . .

Less Money, Fewer Meals

Spending on the cluster of nine domestic food programs rose from $30.3 billion in 1982 to $42.7 billion in 1992 (in 2002 dollars). In the 2002 fiscal year it had fallen to $38.4 billion— less than 2 percent of the entire federal budget. Those numbers reflect drastic reductions over time—the [Ronald] Re-

Food Stamps and Welfare Reform

The 1996 welfare reform legislation had serious consequences for the food stamp program. . . . While food stamps remained a federal entitlement, the 1996 legislation included a number of punitive and racist policies such as eliminating food stamps for immigrants and mandating work requirements for many adults without children. Subsequent reforms added some groups of legal immigrants back onto the rolls, but many remained without access to this vital program.

Welfare reform prompted anti-poverty and immigrant rights organizations to intensify local organizing to improve state food stamp policy and increase access. Many states, particularly with large immigrant populations, adopted their own programs to supplant federal funding for food stamps for immigrants, while others applied for federal waivers to exempt counties with high unemployment rates from work requirements. Despite these efforts, welfare reform resulted in large declines in food stamp enrollment. Participation in the food stamp program plummeted by 7.3 million between 1996 and 2000.

Carson Strege-Flora and Menachem Krajcer,
ColorLines, *Summer 2002.*

agan Administration's cuts in 1981–82 and the cuts mandated by welfare reform in 1996—as well as modest funding increases between 1984 and 1993. "The cuts at the beginning of the Reagan Administration and the '96 cuts were far bigger than the modest increases in intervening years," says David Super, general counsel for the Center on Budget and Policy Priorities. "Funding has recovered partially but is well behind what it would have been had it not been for the cuts."

Food programs for the elderly have suffered a steep decline in federal appropriations after adjusting for inflation. In 2002 the government spent $716.5 million on home-delivered meals and on meals provided at senior centers. Ten years earlier it spent $767.4 million (in 2002 dollars), which explains why all over the country older Americans stay for months on waiting lists for a hot meal delivered to their door. The budget for New York City's home-delivered meals programs illustrates the federal government's fiscal retreat: Twenty years ago Washington funded 80 percent of the program and the city funded the rest. Today the federal government provides less than 20 percent, and city and private sources provide the balance.

Undermining the Food Stamp Program

Because food stamps are an entitlement, spending depends on how many people apply. Currently, that amount is about $22 billion, making food stamps by far the largest federal food program. Food stamps, which date back to 1939, have never been used by 100 percent of all people who are eligible. The high point came in 1994, when 75 percent of all eligible people were on the rolls; the low point was in 1999, when only 58 percent were getting help. "A golden era for the food-stamp program never existed," said Doug O'Brien, vice president of America's Second Harvest. There was a time, though, when government agencies, such as the now-defunct Community Services Administration, sponsored extensive outreach and advocacy programs with the goal of enrolling more people. But after the Heritage Foundation attacked its advocacy work in the early 1980s, enrolling more participants was no longer encouraged, remembers Charles Bell, a VISTA [Volunteers in Service to America] worker at the time.

Participation also depends on how hard states make the application process, and in the 1990s they made it very hard. Unfriendly rules requiring excessive verification, more frequent visits from caseworkers and the need to reapply in person, as well as pressure on the states to reduce their error rates, discouraged many from applying. California, New York and Texas have practically criminalized the process by requiring applicants to be fingerprinted, an action that automatically brands them as potential cheaters. It's hardly surprising that only about half of all eligible residents in those states get food stamps. Receiving food stamps has always carried a stigma— "It's an intentional thing that keeps the program small and saves money," says Agnes Molnar, a senior fellow at New York City's Community Food Resource Center. Food-stamp participation is rising again nationwide, but many states still discourage applicants. In New York City, despite a sharp increase in unemployment, food-stamp use actually dropped between 2001 and 2003. "Low-income people have walked away from the program," O'Brien says.

According to Mathematica Policy Research, the average monthly benefit is $185, but the actual amount varies by family size. For elderly people living alone the average benefit is $50, but for 35 percent of this group, the benefit is only $10 because medical expenses and rent are not high enough to offset their monthly income, usually less than $600 from Social Security's Supplemental Security Income. When Congress reauthorized the food-stamp program last year, a move to increase the minimum benefit to $25 failed. "Because of the obsolescence of the assumptions on which food-stamp levels are based, they are no longer sufficient to prevent or guarantee against hunger," says Janet Poppendieck, a sociology professor at Hunter College in New York City. The food-stamp program assumed that families had 30 percent of their income to spend on food, an estimation that was more realistic when there was a much larger supply of low-income housing. Food stamps were intended to fill in the gap between the 30 percent and the cost of an arbitrarily set thrifty food plan. But today poor families use 50–80 percent of their income on housing and have far less to spend on food. The food stamps they do get are not enough for an adequate diet. So families run out of food before the month ends. That's when they turn to the 50,000 food pantries and soup kitchens across the country, links in an intricate system of food rationing that began as a temporary response to cuts during the Reagan years. . . .

No Political Support

Earlier [in 2005] House Republicans passed legislation that would transform the food-stamp program into a block grant, yet another way of pushing responsibility to the states and letting them decide when and if they have sufficient revenues to feed people. It's a way of converting an entitlement into revenue streams for states. After a few years they can divert money to other programs. It's not hard to imagine what will happen to the needy if the recession and budget deficits continue for several years. At the same time, the Agriculture Department hopes to make it more difficult to qualify for free and reduced-price school lunches, because, it says, some kids are getting cheap lunches even though their families are not eligible. Data, however, show that when more income documentation is required, it reduces participation among eligible children.

Today it's hard to find a champion for the hungry in Congress, much less in the executive branch. Hunger is not seen as a pressing political problem. In January [2005], representatives of food advocacy groups met with Agriculture Secretary Ann Veneman and were told there were no extra dollars for food. "We were told it's going to be a tight budget year," says [David] Beckmann [president of Bread for the World]. "They said there would be no more money for child nutrition, and we had to think about how to do more with the money we've got." Robert Blancato, a food-advocacy group lobbyist, says food programs must be recast to generate Congressional interest. "In this environment, programs need additional buzzwords to survive," he says. "If you can repackage the meal programs so they don't look like meal programs, they have a better chance. There's a whole new priority structure in where the money is going."

Meanwhile, no one in Washington talks much about living wages, increasing the minimum wage, indexing it for inflation or expanding the earned-income tax credit. But living wages are the only solution if people are ever to move toward the self-sufficiency and personal responsibility that politicians and the public demand of them. It's hard to buy food when the money you have goes for ever-increasing shelter costs, health-care because you have no insurance and childcare because there are few low-cost options.

No modern industrial nation should protect the nutritional well-being of its citizens through handouts. But until an outraged public decides that hunger is unacceptable in the richest country in history, there will be more Ellen Spearmans asking why they cannot feed their families.

> "The danger of Africans suffering and dying because they're denied the latest modern technology is much higher than it ought to be."

Genetically Modified Foods Can Reduce Hunger

James K. Glassman

In the following viewpoint James K. Glassman contends that European environmentalists are preventing the world's poor, especially Africans, from growing genetically modified (GM) crops that could make money for poor nations and prevent starvation. Glassman asserts that GM crops can help end hunger because they are resistant to pests and grow faster than traditional grains. However, he argues, African nations will not grow them for export because they know Europe, which fears GM foods, will not buy them. Glassman is a resident fellow at the American Enterprise Institute, a public policy research organization that supports limited government and private enterprise.

As you read, consider the following questions:

1. How long have Americans been eating genetically modified food, according to Glassman?

2. According to the author, why do "sensible environmentalists" like GM crops?

James K. Glassman, "Greens Eat Organic Pears, Africa Starves," *American Enterprise*, December 2002, Copyright 2002 American Enterprise Institute for Public Policy Research. Reproduced with permission of The American Enterprise, a national magazine of Politics, Business, and Culture (TAEmag.com).

3. Why did the president of Zambia decline food aid, as explained by Glassman?

What my colleagues Christopher DeMuth and Steven Hayward have christened "romantic environmentalism" —the view that protecting the environment must override all other concerns—emerged as a big loser at the giant U.N. [United Nations] Earth Summit in Johannesburg during September [2002]. The winner was economic development.

After all, decades of academic research shows that clean air and water are by-products of prosperous economies. In Johannesburg, poor countries said they wanted to get rich. To get there, they need cheap, abundant energy—not the windmills and solar cells the Europeans want to foist on them.

Europeans Oppose Food Progress

Expensive, exotic energy sources are fine for Denmark and France, but not—at least now—for Mozambique and Bangladesh. The conference was not a complete rout, though. While failing to achieve their romantic vision on energy, the Europeans managed to impose an unscientific perspective in another economic sphere—agriculture. Four years ago, Europe slapped a moratorium on any further approvals of genetically modified (G.M.) food products. Americans have been eating G.M. corn, potatoes, and soybeans since the mid 1990s with no adverse consequences. Europeans themselves have had no safety or health problems with the nine G.M. products approved between 1994 and 1998.

In fact, the European Commission's own environmental ministry has indicated it opposes the moratorium. Still, governments of individual European countries have decided to pander to the Greens, who share power in many shaky governing coalitions. As a result, genetically modified foods have been blocked in all of Europe.

Europeans led the agricultural revolutions of the past. Today, much of Europe wants to stop the clock on food progress.

That's fine for them—Europe is rich—but their superstition badly hurts the world's poor.

Discouraging G.M. Farming

Genetic techniques have sped the development of crops that are resistant to pests, that grow faster, that can tolerate bad soils, that don't require as much fertilizer. As a result, about 40 percent of America's corn crop and 70 percent of its soybeans now come from G.M. seeds. Sensible environmentalists like G.M. crops—because they help preserve land, reduce fertilizer use, and keep chemicals out of streams.

The European moratorium, however, has stopped G.M. farming in places like Africa. Why should Africans make an investment in superior G.M. plants if they will be prevented from selling them to a prime export market like the E.U. [European Union]?

Of course, Africans can still use the improved crops at home to feed themselves, can't they? Not necessarily. Greenpeace and other extreme environmental groups have focused desperately on keeping the African continent bio-tech free, spreading horror stories in the process. So far, they are succeeding.

The Moratorium Is Worsening Starvation

The result is that people may be dying unnecessarily. As a famine spread in southern Africa last summer, 13 million people risked starvation. The U.S. pledged 490,000 metric tons of food for the drought-stricken region; about one third of it genetically modified corn. But the president of Zambia— under pressure from Green groups, and worried that if any of the corn were planted it might make his country's crops ineligible for export to Europe—actually turned down the food aid. So corn piled up in warehouses next to starving people.

Andrew Natsios, administrator of the U.S. Agency for International Development, blasted the European environmental romantics during the Earth Summit:

Starvation Is the Enemy

In Africa, hunger and malnutrition are common. There are an estimated 25 to 30 million malnourished children on the continent today. The World Health Organisation (WHO) estimates that 54 percent of child mortality in developing African countries is associated with malnutrition. As many as one third of the children in sub Saharan Africa are said to be stunted because of poor diet, while every day thousands of people die from hunger. Millions of people across the continent are regularly threatened by food insecurity. A further tragedy is that millions of people are forced to live below their full potential because they lack the energy and good health to function at their best.

Access to existing and new technologies in agriculture is clearly a high priority in Africa. Biotechnology is one of the new technologies that has a significant role to play in improving crop production and reducing waste.

Technologies are not an unmitigated blessing, especially when they are first introduced. Cars pollute the air and people are killed in accidents, but few people want to be without an automobile. Agricultural technologies also have negative effects. To make them better requires our human ingenuity. Former U.S. President Jimmy Carter said it so well: "Responsible biotechnology is not the enemy; starvation is."

San Diego Center for Molecular Agriculture/AfricaBio,
"Foods from Genetically Improved Crops in Africa," n.d.

I have never seen, in my 30 years of public service, such disinformation and intellectual dishonesty. . . . It's frightening people into thinking there is something wrong with the food [and] slowing the famine relief in a very disturbing way.

There is more than just environmental romanticism and aversion to sound science behind this. Europeans also have a desire to beat Americans at agribusiness by using non-tariff trade barriers. And it's not just Americans who lose in the process. Genetic technology could eventually allow Africans and Asians to compete with European farmers. Fearing the political power of the farm lobby and the Greens, European politicians would rather placate their former colonies with handouts than buy their goods.

As a result, the danger of Africans suffering and dying because they're denied the latest modern technology is much higher than it ought to be.

| *"You can't solve the problem of hunger by producing more food."*

Genetically Modified Foods Cannot Reduce Hunger

Paul Beingessner

In the following viewpoint Paul Beingessner contends that providing developing nations with genetically modified foods will not solve the problem of hunger. According to him, the world produces enough food to feed everyone. He argues that hunger persists because governments and world agencies fail to make food accessible to the world's poor. Beingessner is a writer and farmer.

As you read, consider the following questions:

1. In the author's opinion, what was the first mistake made by the genetically modified food industry?
2. According to Devinder Sharma, what is the problem of hunger?
3. According to Beingessner, what is lacking in the fight against hunger?

The battle over genetically modified [GM] food continues unabated around the world. In Canada and the USA at this moment, it is focused mainly on Roundup Ready wheat,

Monsanto being first out of the blocks with a GM wheat. In these countries, it is farmers, not environmentalists who are in the forefront. In Brazil and Australia, the fight is largely over the acceptance of GM canola. Again, Monsanto is the leading proponent. The GM industry believes that time is on its side, that the dominos will fall one by one and GM food products will eventually come to be accepted worldwide. After all, everyone needs food, and sooner or later, the stomach will rule. But the GM industry has made a number of mistakes in its bid to win over the world. The first was when it introduced bovine growth hormone, rBGH. This genetically modified hormone was designed to increase milk production in dairy cows. It was accepted in the USA, but Canada and the European Community banned its use, saying that it diminished the health of cows and was not proven safe for humans.

Monsanto's Mistakes

In introducing rBGH, Monsanto erred twice. It introduced a GM product into a food viewed by most consumers to be— and marketed for—its purity and wholesomeness. Not a great first choice. Second, Monsanto sold it on the basis that farmers could, by using it, produce more milk. The problem is, no one in Canada, the USA or Europe had noticed a shortage of milk, wholesome or otherwise. In fact, between 1980 and 2000, the USA government spent $18 billion to sop up huge surpluses of milk to keep prices up. GM wheat falls into a similar category. Wheat prices are chronically low, worldwide. When they begin to rise a bit, some "minor exporter" —like the Ukraine or Kazakhstan—finds a million or two tonnes lying around and prices crash. The plain fact is, you won't see a huge outcry for Roundup Ready wheat to save the world from famine and pestilence. Wheat there is, but hunger persists.

The GM industry does, however, recognize it has a public relations problem with its products. For some years it has proclaimed that GM crops would help the world to tackle its

No Benefits for African Farmers

Considering that genetically modified (GM) products have higher yields than produce from normal hybrid seeds, one may ask why developing countries are worried. A farmer in Malawi does not buy seed; he saves seed from the previous harvest. With GM products such as those advertised by multinational biotechnology corporation Monsanto, he cannot save seed; he will have to buy them each year at higher prices. This farmer is also likely to face marketing problems since certain countries will not accept GM products. The EU [European Union] just lifted the 6-year ban on sale of GM products within the member states earlier this year. But GM as a solution to food security problems among poor countries remains bleak.

Paul Kwengwere, Global Policy Forum, December 30, 2004.

number one problem—hunger. The first of these products was Golden Rice, a rice variety modified to produce beta-carotene, the precursor of Vitamin A. Golden Rice will, it is claimed, reduce Vitamin A deficiency and tackle the problem of blindness induced in parts of the developing world by insufficient Vitamin A intake. Extravagant claims are being made: "Golden rice with beta-carotene and enhanced iron may have a significant impact in reducing malnutrition and premature death."

A Lack of Desire

Indian writer and food policy analyst Devinder Sharma has a simpler take on the problem of hunger. And he might just know: he comes from a country that, together with its neighbors, Pakistan and Bangladesh, is home to half the world's hungry people. The problem, he claims, is not one of a single nutrient lacking. Rather, it is an overwhelming lack of food in the diet of hungry people! Nor is that lack caused by the inability of the world to produce or transport food, as is so often claimed. Rather, it is caused by a lack of desire by governments and world agencies to feed people. "What is being very conveniently overlooked is the fact that what the world's 840 million hungry need is just food, which is abundantly available." Devinder uses a phrase that should shame North Americans and Europeans. He says that if the 320 million hungry in his country only had access to "two square meals" a day, there would be no need for novel foods like Golden Rice.

He points out that India had, in 2001, over 60 million tonnes of foodgrains stored in reserve, much of it open to the weather and subject to spoilage. India, despite any rhetoric to the contrary, seems to have no more interest in feeding the hungry than other, richer countries.

Will the promise of GM crops saving the hungry of the world be the turning point for this technology? Likely not. Oddly enough, you can't solve the problem of hunger by producing more food. There is already enough food in the world. And if farmers were paid decently for producing it, there would be even more. What is lacking is the will by governments to feed the hungry, and the concern by enough of their citizens to force them to do so.

*"Grain-fed cattle, pigs, [and] chickens
. . . are being consumed by the wealthiest people on the planet while the poor
go hungry."*

Reducing the Consumption of Meat Will Help Lessen Hunger

Jeremy Rifkin

In the following viewpoint Jeremy Rifkin asserts that the large amounts of meat consumed in developed nations are worsening the problem of hunger in the developing world. According to Rifkin, land that could be used to grow nutritious vegetables is instead used to grow grain to feed livestock. He concludes that the best way for society to reduce hunger is by promoting a vegetarian diet. Rifkin is the president of the Foundation on Economic Trends.

As you read, consider the following questions:

1. According to Rifkin, what percentage of the grain produced in the United States is fed to livestock?
2. How was Ethiopia using its land during the famine of 1984?
3. What does the author contend is the irony of the food production system?

Jeremy Rifkin, "There's a Bone to Pick with Meat Eaters," *Los Angeles Times*, May 27, 2002. Copyright © 2002, Los Angeles Times. Reproduced by permission of the author.

Hundreds of millions of people are going hungry every day all over the world because much of the arable land now is being used to grow feed grain for animals rather than food grain for people. Grain-fed cattle, pigs, chickens and other livestock, in turn, are being consumed by the wealthiest people on the planet while the poor go hungry.

From Food Grain to Feed Grain

Unfortunately, when agricultural ministers from around the world gather at the U.N. Food and Agricultural Organization's World Food Summit in Rome on June 10 [2002] to discuss how to feed a burgeoning human population, the issue of feed grain versus food grain will not be on the official agenda. It should be. In the past half a century, we have erected an artificial, worldwide protein ladder, with grain-fed beef and other meats on the top rung. Affluent populations, especially in Europe, North America and Japan, devour the bounty of the planet. The transition of world agriculture from food grain to feed grain represents a new form of human evil, with consequences possibly far greater and longer lasting than any past wrongdoing inflicted by men against their fellow human beings. Today, more than 70% of the grain produced in the United States is fed to livestock, much of it to cattle.

Unfortunately, cattle are energy guzzlers, considered by some to be the Cadillacs of farm animals. In the U.S., 157 million metric tons of cereal, legumes and vegetable protein suitable for human use are fed to livestock to produce 28 million metric tons of animal protein that humans consume annually. Cattle and other livestock are devouring much of the grain produced on the planet. This is a new agricultural phenomenon, one that began in the U.S. at the start of the 20th century and spread to other countries after World War II. The transition from forage to feed has taken place with little debate despite the fact that it has had a more pronounced impact on the politics of land use and food distribution than any other single factor in modern times.

Poor Use of Land

In the developing countries, land reform periodically has spawned populist political uprisings. Still, while ownership and control of land have been issues of great public debate, how the land is used has been of less interest. Yet the decision to use the land to create an artificial food chain has resulted in misery for hundreds of millions of people around the world. Bear in mind that an acre of cereal produces five times more protein than an acre devoted to meat production; legumes (beans, peas, lentils) can produce 10 times more protein; leafy vegetables 15 times more protein. The global corporations that produce the seeds, farm chemicals and cattle and that control the slaughterhouses and the marketing and distribution channels for beef are eager to tout the advantage of grain-fed livestock.

In the 1970s, many nations followed the advice of the U.N. Food and Agricultural Organization, which suggested switching to coarse grains that could be more consumed by livestock. World meat production has risen fivefold The shift from food to feed continues apace despite the growing hunger of an increasingly desperate humanity. The human consequences of the transition from food to feed were dramatically illustrated in 1984 in Ethiopia, when thousands were dying each day from famine. The public was unaware that, at the same time, Ethiopia was using some of its agricultural land to produce linseed cake, cottonseed cake and rapeseed meal for export to Britain and other European nations to be used as feed for livestock.

Tragically, 80% of the world's hungry children live in countries with food surpluses, much of which is in the form of feed fed to animals that will be eaten by well-to-do consumers. Thirty-six percent of the world's grain is fed to livestock.

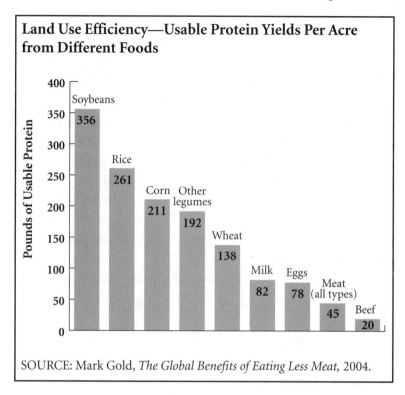

Land Use Efficiency—Usable Protein Yields Per Acre from Different Foods

SOURCE: Mark Gold, *The Global Benefits of Eating Less Meat*, 2004.

In the developing world, the share of grain fed to livestock has tripled since 1950 and now exceeds 21% of the total grain produced. In China, the share of grain fed to livestock has gone from 8% to 26% since 1960. In Mexico, the share rose from 5% to 45%, in Egypt from 3% to 31% and in Thailand from 1% to 30% in the same period.

The Downsides of the Beef Culture

The irony of the food production system is that millions of wealthy consumers in developed countries increasingly are dying from diseases of affluence—heart attacks, strokes, diabetes and cancer—brought on by gorging on fatty grain-fed beef and other meats, while the poor in the Third World are dying of diseases of poverty brought on by being denied access to land to grow food grain for their families.

Consuming large quantities of grain-fed beef and other meats is viewed by many as a basic right and a way of life. The underside of the beef culture, in which displaced people search desperately for their next meal, is rarely considered. There is likely to be plenty of talk at the World Food Summit about how to increase food production. No doubt the biotech companies will be there, touting their genetically modified "wonder seeds." Developed countries and nongovernmental organizations will talk about extending food aid. Other countries will talk about more equitable global trade agreements and securing higher prices for their commodities. There may even be some discussion about the need for agricultural land reform in poor countries.

What is likely to be virtually absent from the debate is talk about the food preferences of the world's wealthier consumers, who favor eating at the highest point on the global food chain while their fellow human beings starve. We are long overdue for a global discussion on how best to promote a diversified, high-protein vegetarian diet for the human race.

> *"The human nutrition value of animal protein is 1.4 times as high as plant protein. This makes it unlikely the world could get more human nutrition if it gave up . . . animal products."*

Reducing the Consumption of Meat Will Not Lessen Hunger

Dennis T. Avery

In the following viewpoint Dennis T. Avery contends that a worldwide shift to a vegetarian diet would not solve the problem of hunger. According to Avery, meat-based diets are more nutritious than are plant-based diets. Moreover, some land is unsuitable for growing high-yield crops for human consumption, but they make good grazing land for cattle, he claims. Avery is the director of the Center for Global Food Issues, a research organization that promotes free trade in agricultural products and supports technological innovations.

As you read, consider the following questions:

1. How has farming shifted the human diet, according to Avery?

2. In the author's view, why are modern crop yields sustainable?

3. Why does Avery believe hunger exists?

Jeremy Rifkin, America's ever-present guilt-monger, says hundreds of millions of people are going hungry because the world's grain crops are being fed to livestock instead of people. Rifkin, writing in the May 27 [2002] *Los Angeles Times*, says eating grain-fed meat is "a new form of human evil." He blames wealthy consumers for "eating at the highest point on the food chain while their fellow human beings starve."

As usual, Rifkin is headed in the wrong direction.

No Vegetarian History

He says, "In the past half a century, we have erected an artificial, worldwide protein ladder, with grain-fed beef and other meats on the top rung."

Shame on Rifkin's history teacher.

There has never been a voluntarily vegetarian society in all history. Our Stone Age ancestors stole wild birds' eggs, gathered clams, and hunted any creature they could club, trap, or spear—to get the vital amino acids and micronutrients that humans need and can't get from plants. Mammoth bones in Wisconsin show not only spear damage—but that the hunters also scavenged meat from long-dead carcasses.

"It's easy to tell from the skeletons of our ancestors whether they were agriculturists or hunter-gatherers," says Arthur De Vany of California State University, an expert on Stone Age diets. "The agriculturists have bad teeth, bone lesions, small and underdeveloped skeletons and small craniums, compared to the hunter-gatherers."

Less Meat Means Worse Health

Rifkin's solution is to force vegetarian diets onto the people of the affluent countries. This would push the world's successful societies toward worse health, without noticeably helping the poor ones. A New York couple was recently arrested for child abuse, because the vegan diet they imposed on their baby had stunted her growth to half the normal size for her 16 months.

An Exodus from Farming

What would actually happen ... if animal husbandry were abandoned in favor of mass agriculture, brought about by humanity turning towards vegetarianism? [According to Brian Carnell:]

"If a large number of people switched to vegetarianism, the demand for meat in the United States and Europe would fall, the supply of grain would dramatically increase, but the buying power of poor [starving] people in Africa and Asia wouldn't change at all.

"The result would be very predictable—there would be a mass exodus from farming. Whereas today the total amount of grains produced could feed 10 billion people, the total amount of grain grown in this post-meat world would likely fall back to about 7 or 8 billion. The trend of farmers selling their land to developers and others would accelerate quickly."

In other words, there would be less food available for the world to eat.

Stephen Byrnes,
Townsend Letter for Doctors & Patients,
January 2002.

The problem for early man was that there weren't enough wild animals to feed many people. The Clovis hunters who came to America about 13,000 years ago hunted dozens of mammal species to extinction, including our native mammoths, horses, camels, and ground sloths.

Ten thousand years ago, humans invented farming to get more food per acre, more reliably, than pursuing wandering herds of elk. But farming shifted the human diet from about 65 percent livestock calories and 35 percent plant calories to 65 percent plants and only 35 percent livestock.

Only in the last 200 years has high-yield farming allowed us to have ample calories to satisfy our kids' hunger (including plenty of livestock calories that optimize growth and cognitive learning) without destroying all the wildlife habitat on the planet.

In fact, the world's farmers are currently feeding twice as many people as we fed in 1950, and giving them much more nutritious diets, from virtually the same cropland base. Modern plant breeding, industrial fertilizers, irrigation, and integrated pest management have tripled the yields.

The Third World has invested far less in agricultural research, and thus has had to clear some tropical forest for additional crops. The tropical countries are also hunting their wild animals to near-extinction for "bushmeat." Hunters in the Congo, for example, are cheerfully selling monkey brains and gorilla steaks.

Crop Yields Are Increasing

Rifkin is right that world meat production has risen fivefold since 1970—but most of the increase has been in the "poor" countries. China's meat consumption, for example, doubled in the 1990s because China's family incomes have soared. Even in "vegetarian" India, three-fourths of the Hindus say they will eat meat (but not beef) when they can afford it.

Modern crop yields are not only the highest in history, but also the most sustainable. Modern farmers have conservation tillage, which eliminates "bare-earth" farming techniques like plowing. It cuts soil erosion by up to 90 percent, often with higher yields because it can double the soil moisture available to the crop plants. (Rifkin is against conservation tillage, because it uses herbicides for weed control.)

Recently, the University of California, Berkeley, engineered biotech plants that not only grow in salty soils, but remove much of the salt—and store it in their leaves. Thus we can harvest the crop, and then harvest the salt for industrial use.

This makes the 40 percent of world food production grown on irrigated land fully sustainable for the first time. (Rifkin is also against genetically engineered crops.)

The Advantages of Modern Farming

Rifkin hates the corporations that support high-yield agriculture. But if corporations didn't take 80 million tons of natural nitrogen [N] from the air each year to fertilize crops, we'd need the organic N from 9 billion cattle instead of the 1.2 billion the world has now. Growing feed for that massive number of cattle might force us to plow down another 30 to 50 billion acres of wildlands.

If corporations didn't make pesticides, we'd lose half of our crop production to pests and have to clear billions more acres of wildlands for cropland.

Farmers grow the feed corn that Rifkin hates for three reasons: (1) the world's natural grasslands are limited and mostly too arid to produce high yields; (2) with high yields, we can grow the "people food" on less land, leaving good grain land available for feed; (3) corn frequently yields 180 bushels per acre, compared with the ten bushels of wheat per acre produced on my Shenandoah Valley farm in 1830. We could grow high yields of alfalfa instead, but alfalfa is harder to store and transport—and not as good for adding pounds to chickens and hogs.

Rifkin should take heart, however. Modern selective breeding has produced animals with much higher feed efficiencies. We also keep many of them indoors, where they're not bothered by heat and cold. And the creatures eat lots of grass and by-products humans can't eat. Thus, in 1997, livestock consumed 74 million tons of human-edible protein and produced 54 million tons of human-food protein—a ratio of 1.4 to 1. As it happens, the human nutrition value of animal protein is 1.4 times as high as plant protein. That makes it unlikely the world could get more human nutrition if it gave up the animal products Rifkin wants us to renounce.

How to Reduce Hunger

He is certainly correct, however, that we should not allow the world's current food situation to persist. Most of the world's poorly fed people are hungry because we haven't yet extended high-yield farming and high-paying off-farm jobs to the whole globe. Africa, in particular, is a building catastrophe for the next two decades, primarily because of its own horrible governance. Nor is the Islamic world doing much better.

Some 800 million people are not getting adequate nutrition consistently. And if we don't triple the yields again, the affluent people will be pitted against the poor and the wildlife. We need more agricultural research to raise the yields and incomes of poor farmers in Madagascar—as well as more exportable grain from Iowa. (Densely populated Asian countries will need to import some of their diet, upgrading as they get richer.)

That means we also need to liberate farm trade. The average tariff on nonfarm products is 4 percent, but in farm products it's 65 percent. The rich countries should import their sugar, and tropical countries can't grow high-yield wheat.

Rifkin says meat is making us too fat. How come he's not crusading against Coca-Cola, Scotch whiskey, and Twinkies?

| *"Ending hunger will require even greater involvement from nonprofit groups."*

Nonprofit Groups Can Help Reduce Hunger

National Anti-Hunger Organizations

Nonprofit organizations can play a significant role in reducing hunger in the United States, the National Anti-Hunger Organizations (NAHO) argue in the following viewpoint. According to the NAHO, these groups enhance government programs by increasing public awareness of the problem of hunger, teaching state and local governments how to take advantage of federal resources, and helping low-income people obtain food assistance. NAHO is a coalition of thirteen organizations, including the Congressional Hunger Center, Food Research and Action Center, and America's Second Harvest.

As you read, consider the following questions:

1. What factors hamper the efforts of government agencies that administer nutrition assistance programs, according to the coalition?

2. According to the coalition, why do some eligible people not participate in federal nutrition programs?

3. As explained by the coalition, what problems do low-income families face after receiving food stamps?

National Anti-Hunger Organizations "A Blueprint to End Hunger," June 3, 2004, pp. 17-18. Copyright © 2004 Alliance to End Hunger. Reproduced by permission of Bread for the World.

Nonprofit groups have a major role to play in ending hunger. While the federal nutrition programs are and should be the primary source of food assistance for Americans at risk of hunger, nonprofits can build public awareness and commitment through effective advocacy. They can also help drive program accountability and improvement as well as deliver services that supplement and enhance our nation's response to hunger.

Hunger affects an individual, then a family and ultimately a community. It can best be seen and understood where it is experienced. Many of the best approaches to addressing hunger arise from local communities. For example, some nonprofits have set up hot lines to help hungry families locate services and food assistance programs.

Working with the Government

On a state and national level, nonprofit groups advocate for the use of government resources in ways that are equitable and effective in meeting the stated purpose of food assistance and related programs. Ending hunger will require even greater involvement from nonprofit groups in advocacy. Meanwhile, emergency food assistance will continue to be needed for local and individual crises as well as for more widespread hunger problems as we transition to a hunger-free America.

Work to increase public awareness of the problem of hunger in the community and advocate for policies that will end hunger. Whether they have a specific anti-hunger focus, nonprofits and charities are some of the strongest voices trying to raise public understanding of the problem of hunger. They conduct analyses and education about hunger in their communities. They advocate for policies that respond to hunger's root causes, such as stronger work supports. They work to ensure full use of government programs and improvements at the local level. They collaborate with government, labor and industry to develop innovative local strategies for connecting eligible people with food assistance programs. They must continue and further improve these efforts.

Ensure that state and local governments take advantage of all federal nutrition assistance programs. Government agencies that administer nutrition assistance programs often are hampered by inadequate resources coupled with complex regulations governing multiple programs. Nonprofit groups can help bring a focus to the issue of hunger and the need for adequate public investments in program administration and infrastructure. Agencies are likely to welcome collaborative efforts with nonprofit groups that can help to increase the reach of nutrition programs.

Helping Needy Families

Educate low-income people about their potential eligibility for nutrition assistance and help connect them with the appropriate programs. Some eligible people do not participate in federal nutrition programs because they find that the time and out-of-pocket costs to enroll and stay enrolled are too high. There are many ways to increase program benefits and reduce costs. . . .

Other people simply do not know they are eligible for benefits. Relatively small investments in outreach can pay large dividends. For example, many nonprofit groups around the country take advantage of their own or government-provided computer screening tools to help families determine whether they are eligible for federal food assistance.

Monitor program performance in food stamp offices, schools and communities. Nonprofit groups can serve an essential role in making sure that nutrition programs are reaching the people who need them and accomplishing the stated objectives. Food stamp offices, schools and communities vary tremendously in their effectiveness in implementing the nutrition programs. In most cases, others can readily replicate the best practices of high performers.

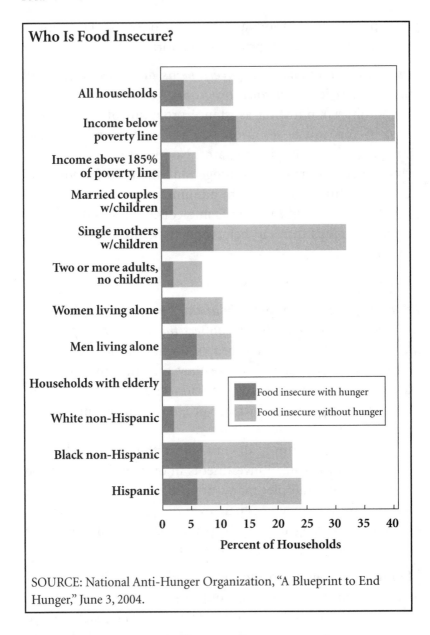

Who Is Food Insecure?

SOURCE: National Anti-Hunger Organization, "A Blueprint to End Hunger," June 3, 2004.

Providing More Food Choices

Ensure that, once families are connected with food assistance, they also have access to affordable nutritious food. Even when low-income families access programs like the Food Stamp

Program that boost their ability to purchase food, they can have difficulty finding affordable markets that carry a wide variety of healthy foods. Supermarkets are scarce in low-income rural and urban communities. Nutritious food, particularly produce, can be difficult to acquire for residents of these communities. Prices at existing supermarkets in poorer neighborhoods typically are higher than in middle-income communities. These factors can have a substantial impact on a family's budget and diet.

To address this situation, many nonprofit groups work in low-income communities to secure new food retail outlets as well as more food choices through community gardens, farmers' markets, farm-to-school sales and cooking education classes. Not only can these projects directly improve people's nutrition, they also bring other benefits to communities and forge alliances with new constituencies, such as farmers.

Continue to acquire and distribute balanced and nutritious food. Expanding the charitable emergency food system cannot bring an end to hunger. Our nation needs to reach the point where all citizens have the means to acquire sufficient quantities of nutritious food. We recognize that it will take some time to get there, and in the interim food pantries, soup kitchens and other programs that provide food to people facing hunger will continue to be needed. Ultimately, emergency feeding should become just that, food for emergency situations.

> *"Under-funded private charities have increasingly been asked to handle many responsibilities performed by government."*

Faith-Based Charities Are Failing to Reduce Hunger

Joel Berg

Private charities lack the resources needed to prevent hunger, Joel Berg argues in the following viewpoint. He contends that cuts in government antipoverty programs have required food pantries and soup kitchens to feed increasing numbers of Americans. However, Berg maintains, these agencies are insufficiently funded and cannot help everyone who is in need. He concludes that charities cannot take the place of government programs. Berg is a leader in the fields of hunger, food security, and community service, and a contributor to Nieman Watchdog, a project supported by the Nieman Foundation that encourages journalists to monitor the actions of people in power.

As you read, consider the following questions:

1. How many people did charities feed in 2001, according to Berg?
2. According to the author, why did forty-eight agencies shut down in 2004?

3. What analogy does Berg use to describe charities that fight hunger?

Does the growing poverty and hunger in America indicate that President [George W.] Bush's Faith-Based and Community Initiative is failing? Has the Administration used the relatively small funding for this initiative to mask broader cuts in anti-poverty programs such as his recent proposal to cut $1.1 billion (over ten years) in food stamps funding?

Do the "armies of compassion"—the people who actually run faith-based food pantries and soup kitchens—believe that they should be [the] nation's first line of defense against hunger, or do they believe that the government should take more of a leadership role in strengthening the safety net and increasing wages?

How many people are fed by such charities—and how much food is provided by them—compared to the number of people fed by federal programs such as food stamps, WIC [Women, Infants, and Children], and school meals? Do the news media give the false impression that these programs are more effective or economical than governmental programs? Do food distribution charities themselves sometimes give the false impression they are more effective than government in order to increase donations to them?

How much money does the government spend giving food to such charitable programs and providing tax breaks to private donors to such programs? Would it be more cost-effective for government to simply expand existing federal nutrition assistance programs?

Increasingly Reliant on Food Pantries

Over the last few decades, under-funded private charities have increasingly been asked to handle many responsibilities performed by government, a trend that has been bolstered by

Charity Camouflages the Truth

Soup kitchens and shelters started as emergency responses to terrible problems—to help ensure that people do not starve, or die from the elements. No one, certainly not their founders, ever considered these services as appropriate permanent solutions to the problems. But soup kitchens and food pantries are now our standard response to hunger; cities see shelters as adequate housing for the homeless. Our church-sponsored shelters can camouflage the fact that charity has replaced an entitlement to housing that was lost when the federally subsidized housing program was gutted twenty years ago. Our soup kitchens can mask unconscionable cuts in food stamps.

David Hilfiker, Other Side, *September/October 2000.*

President Bush's Faith-Based and Community Initiative. Many members of the "armies of compassion" themselves—the people who actually run faith-based food pantries and soup kitchens—believe it is a major mistake to replace a large-scale government safety net with under-funded private charity.

Given that President Bush frequently cites hunger as one of the social ills he wants addressed by his Faith-Based and Community Initiative, this is a good issue upon which to assess whether the Bush initiative is working. As a direct result of the increasing poverty, hunger, and food insecurity—as well as cutbacks in the social service safety net and the exhortations by President Bush and others—America is increasingly relying upon charitable food pantries and soup kitchens to feed low-income Americans.

In 2001, according to America's Second Harvest (the national network of food banks and food rescue organizations that supplies food to such kitchens and pantries), these agencies collectively fed more than 23 million low-income Americans, including more than five million children and nine million seniors. For the first time, the number of Americans utilizing private pantries and kitchens surpassed the number of Americans utilizing government food stamps.

Annual reports from the U.S. Conference of Mayors, as well as reports from local feeding organizations nationwide, indicate that the numbers have soared upwards since then, but we won't know the exact figures until America's Second Harvest releases its updated national study in the Fall of 2005.

Cannot Meet Demand

Pantries and kitchens—most of which are faith-based—are increasingly having trouble meeting the growing demand. For example, in New York City, even before September 11 [2001], more than 1.7 million New Yorkers lived below the federal poverty line (which is a little more than $15,000 for a family of three), and more than one million were forced to utilize charitable pantries and kitchens.

According to the most comprehensive annual survey of local hunger (conducted by my organization, the New York City Coalition Against Hunger), the number of people fed at the city's pantries and kitchens rose by 48 percent from 2000 to 2003. That number rose an additional 9 percent from 2003 to 2004, indicating that any economic recovery has yet to significantly aid the lowest-income New Yorkers. Fully 81 percent of the city's pantries and kitchens said they faced at least some increased demand for food in 2004, with 52 percent saying the demand had increased "greatly."

The number of people being fed by such agencies is now at record levels. Yet, in [2004] only 22 percent of the agencies obtained more food and funding, only 15 percent hired more staff, and only 27 percent obtained more volunteers. In fact, more than twice as many agencies faced cuts in food and money as obtained increases. This "food distribution resources gap" forced a record 48 agencies to shut down entirely. Of the agencies that were able to stay in business, limited resources forced more than half (53 percent) to ration their food by either turning away hungry New Yorkers, reducing portion sizes, and/or cutting hours of operation—a 20 percent increase since 2002 in the number of agencies forced to ration food. (See NYCCAH's 2004 and 2003 Annual Hunger Surveys at www.nyccah.org.)

Goodwill Is Not Enough

While most of these agencies nationwide were founded in the 1980s by volunteers who thought they would be temporary, today there are more than 30,000 such programs across the country, often run by the very same volunteers who started them. In New York City, the number of these charities rose from about 30 in 1980 to more than 1,200 today.

This past Thanksgiving and Christmas, as we do yearly, the nation collectively celebrated these programs as proof of our goodwill and generosity. While the country generally hears little about hunger throughout the year, during the holiday season we were blanketed with Norman Rockwell-like media images of celebrities, political leaders, and average citizens volunteering to feed "the needy."

Yet, as in the case of the original bucket brigades that brought citizens together but failed to put out fires these modern bucket brigades—as heartwarming as they are—are mostly failing. It is no wonder then that the people who run them say it is far more important for elected officials to enact concrete governmental policies to reduce hunger and poverty than to aid charities, according to a survey conducted in the summer of 2004 by my organization, the New York City Coalition Against Hunger.

Periodical Bibliography

America   "Food, Shelter or Medicine?" March 29, 2004.

Barry Bearak   "Why People Still Starve," *New York Times Magazine*, July 13, 2003.

John Buell   "Old Europe and New GM Foods," *Progressive Populist*, July 15, 2003.

Jerry Cayford   "Breeding Sanity into the GM Food Debate," *Issues in Science and Technology*, Winter 2004.

Ross Clark   "What's Good for GM Is Good for the World," *Spectator*, October 25, 2003.

Robert F. Drinan   "Report Shows World Hunger Increasing," *National Catholic Reporter*, April 2, 2004.

Feedstuffs   "Reducing Hunger Would Provide Economic Bounce," December 20, 2004.

Ruth Gadebusch   "Battling Hunger," *Liberal Opinion Week*, August 10, 2005.

Brian Halweil   "The Global Food Fight," *Washington Post National Weekly Edition*, September 29, 2003.

Trudy Lieberman   "Let Them Eat Cake," *Nation*, May 9, 2005.

Stephanie Mencimer   "Green Genes," *Washington Monthly*, September 2003.

Patrick Moore   "The Green Case for Biotech," *American Enterprise*, March 2004.

Wayne Roberts   "Digest This," *Alternatives Journal*, Fall 2003.

Robert Watson and   "Thought for Food," *New Scientist*, August 7,
Beverly Mcintrye   2004.

For Further Discussion

Chapter 1

1. Michael Fumento grants that journalists often exaggerate health scares, but he claims they did not when reporting on mad cow disease. Do you agree with his assessment?

2. After reading the viewpoints on genetically modified foods and irradiated foods, would you be more or less likely to eat these products? Why or why not?

3. After reading the viewpoints in this chapter, how confident are you in the safety of America's food supply? What steps would you take to improve food safety? Please explain your answers.

Chapter 2

1. Most people include meat in their diets. After reading the viewpoints by Matthew Scully, Amy Garber, and James Peters, what steps, if any, would you take to improve the condition of farm animals? Explain your answers.

2. Marika Alena McCauley and Laura Inouye and John J. Miller dispute the healthiness of organic foods. Which author(s) do you believe offers the more convincing argument? Why?

3. Karl Beitel and Dennis T. Avery debate whether farm subsidies are necessary. Whose argument do you find more compelling and why? Are there other policies you would suggest to ensure that farming remains economically viable? Explain your answers.

Chapter 3

1. After reading the viewpoints in this chapter, do you think that obesity is the result of poor personal decisions or factors outside a person's control? Explain your answer.

2. Sharron Dalton and Todd G. Buchholz refer to a lawsuit against fast-food restaurants in their viewpoints. If you were the judge, what decision would you have made in the case? Please explain your answer, drawing from the viewpoints.

3. Richard Berman and Barry Yeoman cite schools as a major factor in obesity. Do you believe schools deserve this blame or should more focus be placed on parents? Please explain your answer.

Chapter 4

1. The authors in this chapter debate the best ways to solve the problem of hunger. Which of the solutions do you believe is most effective? What other solutions would you propose? Explain your answers.

2. Jeremy Rifkin and Dennis T. Avery debate whether people in Western nations should change their eating habits in order to reduce hunger in developing countries. After reading their viewpoints, do you believe Western nations have a responsibility to poorer countries, or should developing nations be more autonomous in solving their food problems? Please explain your answer.

3. The National Anti-Hunger Organizations and Joel Berg disagree on the ability of charities to reduce hunger. Whose argument do you find more convincing and why?

Organizations to Contact

Action Against Hunger USA (AAH)
247 West Thirty-Seventh St., Suite 1201
  New York, NY   10018
(212) 967-7800 • fax: (212) 967-5480
e-mail: info@actionagainsthunger.org
Web site: www.actionagainsthunger.org

Action Against Hunger USA is a wing of Action Against Hunger, an international nongovernmental organization that is a leader in the fight against hunger. The organization provides emergency relief and treatments for malnutrition. AAH publishes the newsletter *Response.*

American Council on Science and Health (ACSH)
1995 Broadway, Second Floor, New York, NY   10023-5860
(212) 362-7044 • fax: (212) 362-4919
e-mail: acsh@acsh.org
Web site: www.acsh.org

ACSH is a consumer education organization that is concerned with issues relating to food and nutrition. It provides consumers with scientific evaluations of food and information on health hazards and benefits. Articles on food safety and publications such as *Irradiated Foods* and *The Role of Beef in the American Diet* are available on the Web site.

American Dietetic Association
120 South Riverside Plaza, Suite 2000
  Chicago, IL   60606-6995
(800) 877-1600
Web site: www.eatright.org

The American Dietetic Association is the largest organization of food and nutrition professionals in the United States. It works to shape the food choices of the public for optimal nutrition and health. The association publishes newsletters for members, as well as the monthly *Journal of the American Dietetic Association* and booklets, fact sheets, and pamphlets about nutrition.

American Obesity Association (AOA)

1250 Twenty-Fourth St. NW, Suite 300
 Washington, DC   20037
(202) 776-7711 • fax: (202) 776-7712
e-mail: pr@obesity.org
Web site: www.obesity.org

The goal of the AOA is to teach society that obesity is a disease and to develop strategies to deal with the epidemic. Its activities include education about and research on obesity. Fact sheets on obesity are available on the Web site.

Animal Agricultural Alliance

PO Box 9522, Arlington, Virginia   22209
(703) 562-5160
e-mail: info@animalagalliance.org
Web site: www.animalagalliance.org

The alliance consists of individuals, organizations, and companies who want to provide consumers with accurate information about the importance of animal agriculture in efforts to feed the world. It provides information on agroterrorism and factory farms. Alliance members have access to newsletters.

Center for Consumer Freedom

PO Box 27414, Washington, DC   20038
(202) 463-7112
Web site: www.consumerfreedom.com

The Center for Consumer Freedom is a nonprofit coalition of restaurants, food companies, and consumers that aims to promote personal responsibility and protect consumer choices. Opinion pieces on food safety and obesity, cartoons, and a daily news archive can be found on the center's Web site.

Food and Agriculture Organization of the United Nations (FAO)

Viale delle Terme di Caracalla
  Rome   00100
  Italy
(+39) 06 57051 • fax: (+39) 06 570 53152
e-mail: FAO-HQ@fao.org
Web site: www.fao.org

FAO is an organization that leads the global effort to fight hunger. It provides information on hunger and provides a neutral forum for all countries to debate hunger policy and negotiate agreements. FAO also helps developing nations improve their agriculture practices. Publications available for purchase from the Web site include *Human Nutrition in the Developing World* and the annual *State of Food and Agriculture*.

Food First/Institute for Food Development and Policy

398 Sixtieth St., Oakland, CA   94618
(510) 654-4400 • fax: (510) 654-4551
Web site: www.foodfirst.org

The goal of Food First/Institute for Food Development and Policy is to eliminate the injustices that cause hunger. The institute believes that hunger persists because hungry people lack the resources to produce or buy food. It supports land reform and sustainable agricultural practices. Its publications include *Food First Backgrounders, News and Views*, books, and fact sheets.

National Institutes of Health (NIH)

9000 Rockville Pike, Bethesda, MD   20892
(301) 496-4000
e-mail: NIHinfo@od.nih.gov
Web site: www.nih.gov

The goal of the NIH is to discover new information that will improve everyone's health. It supports and conducts research and helps spread medical information. The NIH publishes brochures, online fact sheets, and handbooks with information about obesity.

Organic Consumers Association (OCA)

6101 Cliff Estate Rd., Little Marais, MN   55614
(218) 226-4164 • fax: (218) 353-7652
Web site: www.organicconsumers.org

OCA is a nonprofit organization that focuses exclusively on the interests of America's estimated ten million organic consumers. The organization deals with issues such as food safety, genetic engineering, and industrial agriculture. The Web site provides links to news and articles on issues such as irradiation, organic food, and genetically engineered food. The association also publishes the newsletters *Organic Bytes* and *Organic View*.

Organic Farming Research Foundation

PO Box 440, Santa Cruz, CA   95061
(831) 426-6606 • fax: (831) 426-6670
Web site: http://www.ofrf.org/

The foundation is a nonprofit organization that sponsors research on organic farming and disseminates the results to farmers, the public, and policy makers. It publishes the newsletter *Information Bulletin*.

Oxfam America

26 West St., Boston, MA   02111-1206
(617) 482-1211 • fax: (617) 728-2594
e-mail: info@oxfamamerica.org
Web site: www.oxfamamerica.org

Oxfam America is an affiliate of Oxfam International, which is a group of twelve organizations that are working in more than one hundred nations to find solutions to poverty and related issues, such as hunger and famine. Oxfam has worked in disasters and emergency situations for over sixty years. The organization publishes papers relating to hunger and famine, such as *HIV/AIDS and Food Insecurity in Southern Africa* and *Food Aid or Hidden Dumping? Separating Wheat from Chaff.*

U.S. Department of Agriculture (USDA)
1400 Independence Ave. SW, Washington, DC   20250
Web site: www.usda.gov

The USDA's primary purpose is to work with farmers and ranchers. In addition, it also oversees federal antihunger efforts such as the food stamp and school lunch programs. The USDA is also responsible for the safety of meat, eggs, and poultry. Publications available on the Web site include *Food & Nutrition Research Briefs* and *Agricultural Research* magazine.

U.S. Food and Drug Administration Center for Food Safety and Applied Nutrition (CFSAN)
5100 Paint Branch Pkwy., College Park, MD   20740-3835
Web site: vm.cfsan.fda.gov/list.html

The mission of CSFAN is to protect the public's health by guaranteeing that the U.S. food supply is safe, sanitary, and correctly labeled. The center is part of the Food and Drug Administration (FDA), a regulatory agency that is responsible for consumer safety. Papers and congressional testimony relating to food safety are available on the Web site, along with consumer advice.

Bibliography of Books

Francie M. Berg — *Underage & Overweight: America's Childhood Obesity Crisis—What Every Family Needs to Know.* New York: Hatherleigh Press, 2004.

Paul Campos — *The Obesity Myth: Why America's Obsession with Weight Is Hazardous.* New York: Gotham Books, 2004.

Christopher D. Cook — *Diet for a Dead Planet: How the Food Industry Is Killing Us.* New York: New Press, 2004.

Greg Critser — *Fat Land: How Americans Became the Fattest People in the World.* Boston: Houghton Mifflin, 2003.

Sharron Dalton — *Our Overweight Children: What Parents, Schools, and Communities Can Do to Control the Fatness Epidemic.* Berkeley: University of California Press, 2004.

Kathleen Hart — *Eating in the Dark: America's Experiment with Genetically Engineered Food.* New York: Pantheon Books, 2002.

Jeffrey P. Koplan, Catharyn T. Liverman, and Vivica I. Kraak, eds. — *Preventing Childhood Obesity: Health in the Balance.* Washington, DC: National Academies Press, 2005.

Erik Marcus — *Meat Market: Animals, Ethics, & Money.* Boston: Brio Press, 2005.

George McGovern, Bob Dole, and Donald E. Messer	*Ending Hunger Now: A Challenge to Persons of Faith*. Minneapolis: Fortress Press, 2005.
Marion Nestle	*Food Politics: How the Food Industry Influences Nutrition and Health*. Berkeley: University of California Press, 2002.
Marion Nestle	*Safe Food: Bacteria, Biotechnology, and Bioterrorism*. Berkeley: University of California Press, 2003.
Susan Okie	*Fed Up!: Winning the War Against Childhood Obesity*. Washington, DC: Joseph Henry Press, 2005.
Gregory E. Pence	*Designer Food: Mutant Harvest or Breadbasket of the World?* Lanham, MD: Rowman & Littlefield, 2002.
T. Hugh Pennington	*When Food Kills: BSE, E. coli and Disaster Science*. Oxford, UK: Oxford University Press, 2003.
Peter Pringle	*Food, Inc.: From Mendel to Monsanto—The Promises and Perils of the Biotech Harvest*. New York: Simon & Schuster, 2003.
George Pyle	*Raising Less Corn, More Hell: The Case for the Independent Farm and Against Industrial Food*. New York: Public Affairs, 2005.

C. Ford Runge et al.   *Ending Hunger in Our Lifetime: Food Security and Globalization.* Baltimore: Johns Hopkins University Press, 2003.

Eric Schlosser   *Fast Food Nation: The Dark Side of the All-American Meal.* New York: HarperCollins, 2002.

Loretta Schwartz-Nobel   *Growing Up Empty: The Hunger Epidemic in America.* New York: HarperCollins, 2002.

Jeffrey M. Smith   *Seeds of Deception: Exposing Industry and Government Lies About the Safety of the Genetically Engineered Foods You're Eating.* Fairfield, IA: Yes Books, 2003.

Morgan Spurlock   *Don't Eat This Book: Fast Food and the Supersizing of America.* New York: G.P. Putnam's Sons, 2005.

Steve Striffler   *Chicken: The Dangerous Transformation of America's Favorite Food.* New Haven, CT: Yale University Press, 2005.

Mark L. Winston   *Travels in the Genetically Modified Zone.* Cambridge, MA: Harvard University Press, 2002.

Index